Sikkim Himalaya

Sikkim Himalaya
Travels in the Cloud Kingdom

David Lang

First published 2003 by Pomegranate Press,
Dolphin House, 51 St Nicholas Lane, Lewes, Sussex, England BN7 2JZ
    email: pomegranatepress@aol.com

Cover photograph: Pandim from the trail
Back cover (clockwise from top left): Blood pheasant; *Meconopsis horridula*; family at the hot springs, Yume Samdong;
    Rheum nobile; lamas playing rhakdong; rainbow over the Tista
Half title page: Pandim
Title page: Tsokha

ISBN 0-9533493-7-3

Books by the same author: *Orchids of Britain* (Oxford University Press, 1980), *The Wild Flower Finder's Calendar*
    (Ebury Press, 1983), *The Complete Book of British Berries* (Threshhold Books, 1987), *A Guide to the Orchids of
    Great Britain and Ireland* (Oxford University Press, 1989) and *Wild Orchids of Sussex* (Pomegranate Press, 2001)

Set in Palatino and New Berolina

Colour origination and printing by Viscan Graphics, 40 Mimosa Road, Singapore 808002

Contents

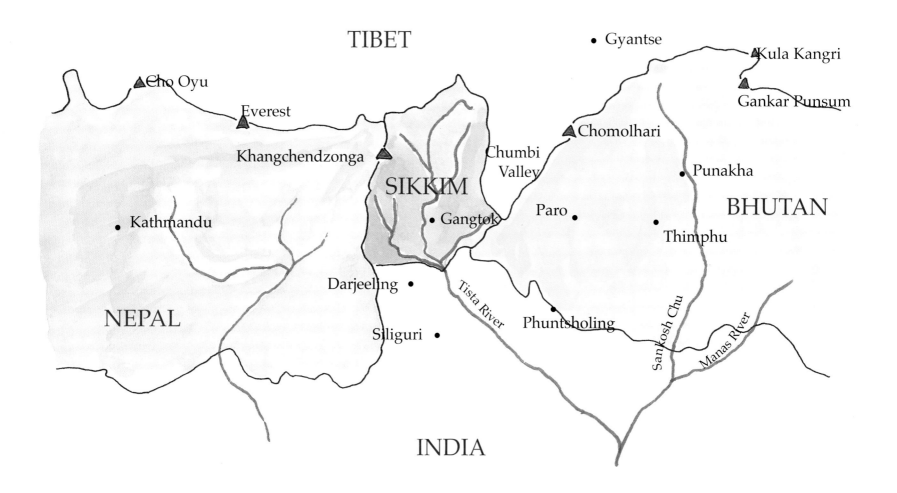

TIBET

Cho Oyu

Everest

Gyantse

Kula Kangri

Gankar Punsum

Khangchendzonga

Chumbi
Valley

Chomolhari

SIKKIM

Punakha

Kathmandu

Paro

BHUTAN

Gangtok

Thimphu

Darjeeling

NEPAL

Tista River

Phuntsholing

Sankosh Chu

Manas River

Siliguri

INDIA

Prelude

Gentiana prolata

Hippophaea salicifolia

'No problem!'

Such a simple and beguiling statement, but one capable of striking dread into the heart of the seasoned traveller, especially in India. The speaker certainly means well, and may even nurture a shrivelling hope that there is indeed no problem, but experience dictates otherwise. There *is* a problem. It is large, probably insuperable, and is going to take up a great deal of your time and patience.

If you can get your own 'No problem!' in first, the result will usually be a big grin. Your adversary knows that you understand the rules of the game, and you are half-way to a solution.

I admit that I have fallen in love with Sikkim, both the country and its people. Mountain people the world over have the capacity to look down, in every sense of the word, on those who dwell at a lower altitude. The natural circumstances of their situation make them tough and self-reliant, splendid people to have as companions when things go wrong, which they have a habit of doing if one is travelling in a remote area blessed with extremes of climate. The local people have an innate kindness which makes them treat westerners, especially people like botanists, with the amused condescension we usually reserve for the very old, the very young and the harmlessly insane. Add to that a robust but by no means naive sense of humour, the capacity to laugh uproariously at life the worse the circumstances become, and you have a most endearing people.

This is not to say that everything is wonderful. Like most countries Sikkim has had its share of problems, but those which influence the traveller are mainly the product of the contorted geography and seasonally awful weather which are peculiar to the eastern Himalaya.

My interest in the Himalaya was first stimulated as a child, listening to my father reading aloud from the works of the botanical explorers Reginald Farrer, Frank Kingdon-Ward and 'Chinese' Wilson. In my mind's eye I could see the high mountains, the valleys carpeted with primulas and gentians, and, above all, the yaks. There was something about yaks which appealed to a

Taktsang

small child, and I longed one day to see them and the flower pastures where they lived.

My Himalayan dreams had to remain unfulfilled. Post-war restrictions on foreign travel and then family circumstances meant that there was little prospect of following in the steps of my botanical gods. In the summer of 1983 I finally got the chance to travel to the Himalaya on a trek to Kashmir and Ladakh, led by the legendary botanist Oleg Polunin. There at last I saw what I had only dreamed about, great snow peaks, glaciers and the flower-studded meadows of my imagination. Returning home I felt sure that I had fulfilled my ambition and purged the Himalayan bug from my system, when in reality it had settled in happily to become an obsession.

Two years later I travelled as part of a trekking expedition to the Kingdom of Bhutan in the eastern Himalaya. This was a journey to the north-west of the country, a truly magical experience, interrupted by a dramatic and unexpected change in the weather. We had crossed over a high pass – the Nyeli La (4780m) – into the beautiful valley of Lingshi north-east of Chomolhari, where we spent two days exploring, including a fascinating glacial valley to the foot of Jitsu Drake. On our way back into camp on the second day we noticed heavy cloud building up in the south-east. The next morning we started to climb up the Chabeychang Chu in heavy drizzle on our planned route which would have taken us over the high Yali La to the capital Thimphu.

At about 4500m the pack yaks caught up with us, and in the worsening weather we decided to camp, as several of the party were exhausted and suffering from altitude sickness. All able hands then set about erecting tents, only to find that the yak men had used our sleeping mats as yak blankets, and that they were sodden. Conditions were now foul, with driving snow, so we all retreated into our sleeping bags fully clad, our breath freezing on the inside of the tents.

The night that followed was horrible. I awoke to find something pressing down on my face, the tent collapsing under the weight of the snow. Cries for help were heard, and several of us crawled out in the blizzard to find other tents flattened, burying their occupants, who had to be dug out and evacuated to those which were still standing.

By morning over one metre of snow had fallen. We ate a scratch breakfast standing in the mess tent, and then set off again with the yaks, heading for the Yali La. Conditions soon became bad, with driving snow which covered the path to a depth of more than a

The summit of the Nyeli La

Indian pond heron

Lingshi Dzong

metre in places. Merely finding the track was a problem, and the fitter members ploughed ahead to break a trail and encourage the yaks to follow. We struggled on until noon, when a virtual white-out and very deep snow prevented further progress. Unable to see any geographical features and never having done the route before, our guides were lost, although our altimeters told us that we were barely 150m below the pass. We were unable to have any food, because all the supplies were packed on the yaks, and there was no chance to make anything hot. All our footwear was soaked by snow and repeated wading across streams and rivers we could not see under the snow, so we were forced to retreat. By this time the yaks, which had been forging chest deep through the drifts like hairy snow-ploughs, decided this was a daft game to play and turned tail, disappearing

down the valley with all our camping gear. The retreat to Lingshi was a nightmare, as we staggered down in the deep snow and fading light, reaching the shelter of a stone walled shed in a state of exhaustion. The temperature dropped to -15°C, so after drinking some hot sweet tea, we crawled into our damp sleeping bags.

It was a cold and chastened group which emerged from the relative warmth of our sleeping bags the next morning. All our faces were red and puffy from snow burn, but everyone had recovered relatively well. Very little fuel was available, and we were forced to demolish a wooden privy being constructed for tourist use in order to make a fire to dry our gear, as every single item was soaking wet. Water had even penetrated cameras and lenses. The shed was draped with lines of clothing hung up to dry, while everyone was busy trying to dry the more delicate pieces of equipment.

Our porters and camp staff had not fared so well. Two camp staff, the cook, the Tibetan yak man and his little boy were prostrated with snow blindness. None had expected snow at this time of year, so none had brought snow goggles, although they did possess them. I cleaned up their eyes, dressing them with anaesthetic eye ointment and pads of clean toilet paper, (soaking wet and ice cold), and then bandaged them, giving them paracetamol to ease their misery. I am by profession a veterinary surgeon, which evoked some rueful laughter from the sufferers when they found out. I don't think that the yak man and his little boy had ever had their faces washed before in their lives.

The passes were effectively blocked by 1.5–2m of snow, so that we could not walk out, and several of our party were too ill even to have attempted it. Food and fuel were both in very short supply, as we had planned to pick up supplies once we were over the Yali La for the return walk to Thimphu. We were trapped in Lingshi.

Our guide set off to try to reach an army post up on the mountain above us, so that a message could be sent to the capital requesting a helicopter to evacuate our party. In the event it took him three and a half hours to reach the post, virtually swimming in places through snow up to his armpits, and the message was duly transmitted. Later two soldiers struggled down from Lingshi dzong with a welcome load of dry firewood. We learned from them that we could expect a return message next morning. In the evening two Tibetans from Lingshi village came up to the camp. On the night of the storm the yaks suddenly turned up around 10.30 pm, having run all the way from the pass to their home villages. The local people assumed that the yak men must have died, since the animals had appeared without them.

The next morning dawned cold and crystal clear, one of those magical mornings which make all the discomfort worthwhile. Around us was a fairytale world of ice and snow, the peaks of Jitsu Drake and Tshering Gang so clear that you felt that you could reach out and touch them. We learned that it might be possible for a helicopter to land on a small hill several kilometres from our camp, where there was less danger of the vibration of the rotor blades setting off an avalanche of the freshly fallen snow. This meant that we had to beat a path from our camp to the chorten at the head of our valley, and then up to the proposed landing site.

Jitsu Drake [Sir Edward Peck]

Above: The retreat from Yali La

Below: A helicopter comes to the rescue

This was hard work, since despite the fierce sun the snow had frozen hard. Beside the track we found the paw prints of snow leopard leading all the way up to the chorten, as well as the slots of musk deer crossing our path in several places. Beside us as we worked we watched tiny Pallas's warblers and flocks of black tits.

In the afternoon I witnessed an amazing passage of birds of prey coming off the Tibetan plateau and flying west along the ridge over the Lingshi dzong. One after the other a procession of birds glided high overhead, silvery pallid harriers, tawny eagles, lammergeiers, black and white Himalayan griffon vultures, sparrowhawks, and white-throated needle-tails, a species of swift. The procession went on for well over three hours.

We had enough wood of one sort or another to keep a reasonable fire going, but food was in short supply. The Dungpa in charge of Lingshi dzong, Tshewang Rinzin, came down to visit us, a cheerful, stocky Bhutanese, and a good organiser. He had made direct contact with the Indian military on his own initiative once he learned of our predicament, and there were hopes that if the good weather held it might be possible to arrange a series of helicopter flights to lift us out.

The next day was fine, enabling three flights to be made. The extreme altitude caused considerable problems for the pilot, who could lift off with only two passengers at a time, and had further difficulty turning and climbing out of the steep-sided valley. Finally all remaining trek members were lifted out, and we reassembled in Thimphu after the dramatic flight from Lingshi, down the Mo Chu to Paro.

Only then did we start to appreciate the complexity of the rescue operation which had lifted us to safety. We learned that a massive storm had hit the eastern Himalaya, bringing heavy snowfall and devastating landslips to a huge area. It is all too easy, when you are stuck and isolated as we were, to lose sight of the problems faced on the other side of the mountains by your would-be rescuers. The authorities were inundated with calls for help from every quarter, including a Japanese climbing expedition attempting Kula Kangri and an irate Indian VIP stranded by a landslide near Ha in southwest Bhutan.

The helicopter had to come from India, with all the diplomatic problems that entailed, while a tanker load of aviation fuel had to be driven up from the plains along a road blocked repeatedly by landslides triggered by the heavy snowfall. Several slides had to be dynamited to clear them. Never before had the Bhutanese government needed to mount such an operation, and it is to their eternal credit that it was done so quickly and efficiently. It must have given them cause to rethink their attitude to the development of tourism.

On the return journey to Bagdogra airport we drove past fields full of egrets and pond-herons, past telephone wires with drongos, bulbuls, rollers and kingfishers perched on them, to the inevitable tedious wait at the airport for the flight to Delhi. On the wall of the reception area I noticed some very attractive posters extolling the virtues of Sikkim, the Cloud Kingdom, with photographs of wonderful mountain peaks, flower-filled meadows and gorgeously decorated Buddhist temples.

'Welcome to Sikkim,' they said.

Tawny eagle (Aquila rapax) [Tony Heald/Nature Picture Library]

The Geography of Sikkim

Rhododendron roylei

After my return from Bhutan, I at last did something I should have done years before, and joined theAlpine Garden Society (AGS). With all the bumph one receives as a new member came a back copy of the quarterly bulletin, featuring two expeditions made by the AGS to north-west Sikkim in 1983. The first party travelled out in June, journeying from Yuksam up to the Goecha La east of Khangchendzonga, and also to Bikhbari on the approach to the peaks of Rathong and Kabur. The second party returned in September along the same route, with the main aim of gathering seed from sites marked on the initial trip. I read the articles by Chris Brickell, Mike Upward, Brian Mathew and Barry Starling with rising excitement. The photographs of the plants they found were beautiful, while the problems they experienced with officialdom, weather and leeches I tended to push to the back of my mind.

Ranunculus adoxifolius

Caltha palustris var.*himalensis*

Khangchendzonga

In the spring of 1986 I was asked to lead a trekking party along the same route as that followed by the AGS. I was soon immersed in reading every scrap of information I could glean on Sikkim, and found it to be very sparse indeed. Barry Starling was very helpful in supplying me with plant lists and details of the places they had visited. Mike Upward had wryly observed 'Maps of Sikkim are rather a joke,' not only for the absence of meaningful data, but for their mind-boggling diversity in the spelling of place names. Yuksam appears in various guises as Yoksun, Yoksam and Yoksum, and Bakhim as Bakkhim, Bakkim and Buckeem. The name for a village or geographical feature could be utterly different, depending upon whether the person asked was a Lepcha, Bhotia or Nepali.

Good maps of the northern areas exist, but are not generally available, so one is forced to work with maps drawn up any time from the turn of the century to the early 1940s. It says a great deal for the skills of the early cartographers that the details shown are so accurate. It was no fault of theirs that country so steep and rugged meant that contour lines were inevitably crowded close together, so that simple black and white maps are very hard to read.

Since the maps were drawn there has been an extensive development of the system of roads and bridges, few of which appear on the old maps. Sometimes the road will follow on the opposite side of a river valley to that depicted on the map, the original having been swept into oblivion by landslides.

Sikkim is roughly rectangular in outline: 100km long from north to south and 80km wide. It was formed from a huge dome of metamorphic rock stretching from Nepal to Bhutan, which was squeezed out southwards by the collision of the Indian sub-continent as it moved under the Tibetan plateau. The fossil-bearing sediments from the bed of the prehistoric Tethys Sea have come to lie on top of the mountains of north Sikkim, pushed up to over 8000m and still rising. The dome has been shaped by the catchment of the Tista Chu, which runs from the northern border right down through the middle of Sikkim. To the west the land climbs up to the Singalila Ridge, forming the border with Nepal and running up to the great mass of Khangchendzonga (8598m) with its five main peaks. Lying in Sikkim's north-west corner, Khangchendzonga lies south of the true Himalayan chain, and is composed of hard wearing gneiss.

From there the northern border with Chinese-occupied Tibet starts from the pass of the Chorten Nyima La (5795m) just east of Khangchendzonga, via the Kongra La (4505m), north of the mighty peaks of Khangchengyao (6889m) and Gurudongmar, to the Say Say La 80km to the east. There are few negotiable passes through this massive northern barrier to the Tibetan plateau, and those that do exist are closed by snow for much of the year.

Landslides are a common feature on the banks of the Tista and Lachung rivers

The confluence of the Rangit Chu and Tista Chu

The eastern border abuts on to the Chumbi Valley for much of its length, from the peak of Pauhungri and the Donkya La (5520m), south to the passes of the Natu La and Jelep La, and the border with Bhutan.

The Tista river rises near the Donkya La and circles north of Khangchengyao before starting its descent of nearly 5000m in scarcely 100km. The other main tributary, the Lachung Chu, also rises near the northern border, uniting with the Tista at Tsunthang in a deep gorge. These valleys, with that of the Prek Chu, are typically U-shaped glacial valleys, formed as the glaciers retreated. Sikkim has one of the wettest climates in the world, with an average rainfall in the capital Gangtok in excess of 5000mm, most of which falls during the monsoon period from May to September. All this water is concentrated into the Tista and Lachung rivers, which cut down through the soft mica schists and shales like a knife through butter, leaving sharp peaks and deep, steep-sided river valleys, which are forever crumbling and easily denuded of their vegetation.

All this has a disastrous effect upon human efforts to build and maintain roads and bridges. Massive landslips are an almost daily occurrence in the wet season, carrying all before them. It is a tribute to the road gangs and engineers that any transport system is maintained at all. The advent of the four-wheel drive jeep has revolutionised travel in Sikkim, but whether you actually reach your destination will depend not only upon luck, but on the skill of your local driver. I have never worked out whether these heroes have nerves of steel or no nerves at all, but I have frequently had to shut my eyes and resort to prayer.

The southern border of Sikkim is formed by the junction of the Tista Chu with the Rangit Chu from the west and the Rishi Chu from the east. North-east of Rinchenpong, on the east side of the Rangit Chu, hot springs emerge in the valley floor, with further springs 4km north-west of Ralong on the west bank of the river. Other hot springs, which I have visited, are found in the north-east of Sikkim 2km west of Yume Samdong on the track up to the Sebu La and at Momay 2km below the glaciers of Khangchengyao.

The border crossing at Rongphu on the Rangpo Chu in the south lies at low altitude in tropical rain forest, hot and steamy, with wild bananas growing in the less accessible stream gullies which carve down the mountainsides. Intensive agriculture dominates this part of Sikkim, with hillsides terraced for the growing of paddy rice, extensive forests of teak and sal, tea gardens on the higher ridges, and a mosaic of small fields for the cultivation of valuable crops such as ginger and cardamom. Cattle and buffaloes are kept for milk, butter and cheese, but this is essentially a peasant agriculture, the plots being small and frequently divided by complex laws of inheritance.

There are few towns and villages in a sense that a westerner would envisage them, but houses are scattered over the steep terraced hillsides like grains of rice on a crumpled green carpet. The extensive forests that 19th century travellers such as Joseph Hooker knew have long gone, cleared for agricultural purposes and for access. Most of the centres of population north of Rongphu lie along the main highway, which twists and turns for 30km

Left: The Tista valley near Mangan

Coelogyne cristata

Rice paddies

Spiranthes sinensis

Facing page: Rheum nobile

Yaks at Yume Samdong

north to the capital Gangtok, built on a hill-top at 1870m. The road then leads north again to Mangan, the government centre for the northern region, and on to Tsunthang at the junction of the Tista and Lachung rivers. Finally a road has been built up each of the river valleys to the northern border with Tibet. Other roads lead east from Gangtok to the Natu La and Jelep La, and west to the border with Nepal.

The extraordinarily rapid rise in altitiude of the country from the border at Rongphu northwards gives this small country a unique diversity in its plant life. From the border to 1500m is mixed tropical rain forest. The next zone is temperate forest stretching up to 3500m, which is the upper limit of the tree zone, although at Tsunthang this only extends to 3000m. It is probable that Sikkim possesses more than 600 species of orchids, many of which are epiphytic and found in the tropical and temperate forests. These include *Dendrobium*, *Coelogyne*, *Pleione* and terrestrial orchids such as *Cypripedium*, *Paphiopedilum*, *Platanthera* and *Ponerorchis*, an astonishingly rich orchid flora in such a relatively small area.

The alpine zone extends from 3000m to 4500m, where it meets the permanent snow line. The change here is from fir to juniper and rhododendron, Sikkim boasting more than 40 species of rhododendron. The alpine plants are spectacular, including many species of *Primula*, *Gentiana* and *Meconopsis*. One of the special alpine plants I particularly love is the giant rhubarb *Rheum nobile*. The flowering spike can grow to 2m tall, clad in huge, creamy white overlapping bracts, like giant handkerchiefs. The story goes that during the Younghusband expedition to Lhasa in 1904 a platoon of soldiers, advancing through the mist, thought that they were about to be ambushed by Tibetans, whose dress included a white shirt. They fired volley after volley at the ghostly figures and, when checking next morning for the bodies of their enemies, found an awful lot of shredded rhubarb.

The rapid rise of the land from Gangtok northwards is also reflected in the change of crops, with barley and hill rice grown in the place of paddy rice. Cabbage growing has been introduced on a large scale around Lachung. The lower montane areas, now denuded of forest, are given over to sheep, goats and yak. Much of the northern region lies almost beyond the monsoon shadow, having a dry bleak climate like that of the Tibetan plateau, bitterly cold in winter, windy and dessicated by the intense sunlight in summer. Here the population is

sparse, consisting mainly of yak herders, who move up to the high valleys to take advantage of the summer grazing.

In recent years the development of hydroelectric schemes has grown rapidly, but the engineering problems posed by unstable rock strata and the risk of earthquake are considerable. Sikkim has also made great strides in developing its tourist industry. The country is incredibly beautiful, with a predominantly Buddhist culture, which retains much that has been destroyed in Tibet during the Chinese Cultural Revolution. The wildlife is diverse, and is still not fully documented. Sikkim has 500 species of birds, 700 species of butterflies, and rare mammals such as the red panda, tiger, brown and blue bears, snow

Top: Joseph Hooker's drawing of Ovis ammon near Khangchengyao [RBG Kew]
Above: Red panda (Ailurus fulgens) at rest in a tree [Jose B. Ruiz/Nature Picture Library]

leopard, bharal (blue sheep), nyan (a sub-species of Marco Polo sheep) and kiang (wild ass).

The very remoteness of the country and the fact that access has been denied to travellers for so long combine to increase its attractiveness to modern tourists. Much of the northern part of Sikkim remains a restricted military zone closed to all foreigners, the product of India's deep and well-merited distrust of the Chinese government. Unless something very extraordinary changes the political climate, these problems are likely to remain or even intensify. Regrettably this has meant that very little field study has been made of the fauna and flora, particularly of the northern half of Sikkim.

It is absolutely essential that a thorough understanding of this remote area is achieved as soon as possible, before military activity or unfettered tourist development destroys one of the few remaining truly wild parts of the Himalaya. Already bodies such as the Sikkim Nature Conservation Foundation are trying to address the problem. To the west they have seen the damage done to the ecosystem by massive tourist development in Nepal, while eastwards they have observed how Bhutan's strict control of limited tourist numbers is functioning. We can only pray that wise counsels will prevail over economic demands for increased revenue from tourism.

Snow leopard (Panthera unthia) [Lynn Stone/Nature Picture Library]

Pandim from Netuk House, Gangtok

History and Exploration

Sikkimese snuff box

The history of Sikkim and, indeed, the manner in which everything proceeds to the present day, is closely bound up with religion. It plays a vitally important role at every level.

Buddhism reached Tibet from India early in the 7th Century AD, and spread to Sikkim much later. The Tibetan ruler Srong-Tsen-Gompo had married two wives, a Chinese princess and a Nepalese princess. Both of them were fervent Buddhists, and they persuaded their husband to send to India for Buddhist books and religious teachers. In time schisms arose within the country, and the Mahayana doctrine led to the acceptance of mythology and mysticism, admitting within the pantheon of the gods the very demons of more primitive religions whose followers it had originally sought to convert.

Lamaism dates from the 8th century, and was founded by Padma Sambhava, the Guru Rimpoche. It may be defined as a mixture of Buddhism with mythology, mysticism and magic. The doctrine of incarnate lamas is more recent.

The Buddhist monk Atisha visited Tibet in the 11th century, where he founded the Kahdampa sect, which insisted on celibacy and abstinence. He strongly deprecated the practice of magic, but three centuries later the practice had become less ascetic and more ritualistic under the title of Gelukpa. The unreformed residue was called Nyingmapa.

The modern recorded history of Sikkim begins in the mid-17th century with the coming of Gyalwa Lhatsun Chempo, regarded as the patron saint of Sikkim. His advent, with that of two other lamas, Ngadak Sempa Chempo and Kathok Rigzin Chempo, fulfilled prophecies that had been made centuries earlier by Guru Rimpoche. In 1641 these three ascetic lamas met at Yuksam, the literal meaning of which in the Lepcha language is 'the meeting place of three lamas'. There they prayed and meditated for many days. They then summoned Phuntsog Namgyal and, in an elaborate consecration ceremony, installed him as the first Chogyal (ruler) of Sikkim. As Dharma Raja he was the founder and ancestor of the present Namgyal dynasty of Sikkim.

The three lamas and the Chogyal ruled over the whole country. Collectively referred to as 'Naljor Cheshi', the four revered yogic brothers, they are worshipped with deep veneration.

Gangtok early in the 20th century

25

The Lepchas are the indigenous people of Sikkim, a Mongoloid race who probably originated in Tibet. Their own name for themselves is 'Rong-pa', which translates as 'the dwellers in the ravines'. They are hunter-gatherers, with a limited 'slash and burn' agriculture, but are renowned for their skill as hunters and for their great knowledge of the medicinal uses of plants. The census of 1981 calculated the population of Sikkim as 11,000 Bhutias and Lepchas, 3,500 Tsongs and 16,000 of Nepalese extraction. Since that time the relative percentage of the indigenous Bhutia–Lepchas has decreased, while that of the Nepalese has increased.

Following the installation of Phuntsog Namgyal in 1641, there was an easing of hostility between Lhasa and Sikkim, and the lamas of Sikkim accepted the authority of the Dalai Lama in matters of religious discipline and procedure. The rajas found that there were benefits in trading with Tibet, and Tibetan became the language at court. Under the influence of Tibet the rajas were induced to move the centre of government to the Chumbi valley. Family feuds in the early 18th Century led to the Bhutanese invading east Sikkim in 1700–1706, and by the 1770s they had taken over much of the country east of the Tista river, after which they were driven out except for the area around Kalimpong.

During the 18th century the Hindu warlords of Nepal harried south-west Sikkim, rustling cattle and taking slaves, until British intervention in 1817 halted their incursions from Darjeeling and the terai west of the Tista. At the end of the Gurkha War, the Treaty of Titalya in 1817 restored all the terai to Sikkim and established the Sikkim rajas as overlords. In 1834 Lepcha malcontents from Nepal made a raid on the tract of lowland terai in the south of Sikkim ceded in 1817, but again pressure from the British forced them to return to Nepal.

The Government of India secured Darjeeling and some of the country immediately surrounding it from the Sikkim raja. At this time the population had risen rapidly from about a hundred to nearly 10,000 with the development of the site as a hill station to which the British administrators and their families could escape from lowland India during the worst of the summer weather.

In 1848 the British botanist Joseph Hooker was persuaded by Dr Falconer, the superintendent of the botanic garden in Calcutta, that he should visit the Himalaya to study and record the flora and fauna. At that time the superintendent of the Darjeeling hill station was Dr Campbell, with whom Hooker stayed and with whom

Sikkimese gentry and ladies, early 20th century

he became firm friends. They planned to travel west of Khangchendzonga to Tibet, and set off in October 1848, returning via west Sikkim in January 1849.

In the following May they made an incredible journey up through Sikkim, first to Lachen and the Zemu valley, and then from Thanggu north-east to Phalung. Returning to Tsunthang at the confluence of the Tista and Lachung rivers, they then journeyed up the whole length of the main valley, looking at several side valleys and high passes, to the Donkya La, ascending to the Tibetan plateau east of Khanchengyao. They then travelled round north of the mountain, past the lake of Tso Lhamo, to Donkung, and so back down the Tista and to Darjeeling. The journey alone was a formidable task, but to make matters worse they were captured and imprisoned under very unpleasant conditions by Donyer Namguay, also referred to as the Pagla Dewan or Mad Prime Minister. This was done despite the fact that they were travelling with the full consent of the Sikkim raja. Far from mad, the Pagla Dewan was using them as hostages to force the government of India to relinquish the right to extradite from Sikkim criminals who had fled there from West Bengal.

In his Himalayan Journals of 1854, Hooker graphically describes the horrendous conditions of their captivity, which were particularly harsh for Dr Campbell. They were finally released and, as a punishment, the Indian government annexed the entire terai and part of central Sikkim. Despite all of this, Namguay continued to wield considerable influence, harbouring wanted criminals and kidnapping British subjects, who were then sold as slaves to Bhutan. In

HOOKER REVISITED

Joseph Hooker made copious drawings during his 1848–49 trip to Sikkim, and published his Himalayan Journals in 1854. The three pairs below match his sketches with the author's photographs.

Top to bottom: Khangchendzonga and Pandim from Dzongri; Glacial boulder at Thanggu; and the Lachung Valley. [Hooker drawings RGB Kew]

Joseph Hooker [RGB Kew]

His Excellency Maharaja of Sikkim, Sir Tashi Namgyal, with his bride, Sikkimese and Tibetan dignitaries, late 19th century

Joseph Hooker plant collecting in Sikkim, 1849

1860–61, with patience exhausted, a force under Col Gawler, with Ashley Eden as Envoy, advanced to the Tista, and in 1861 the Treaty of Tumlong was concluded. British forces were allowed to make a road into Sikkim, and the seat of government was moved back from Tumlong to Gangtok. Slavery was abolished, and basic surveys were undertaken.

In the cold season of 1873-74 Sir John Edgar, then the deputy commissioner in Darjeeling, journeyed through Sikkim and visited all the passes of the Chola Range bordering on the Chumbi valley. Meetings were held with chief officials and with some Tibetan officers from the district of Phari, with the aim of opening up trade via Sikkim to Tibet. At that time the Chinese were in control of Tibet, with a Resident or Ampa in Lhasa. They were jealous of the attempt by the British government to trade with Tibet, and warned the deputy commissioner not to attempt to cross the Chola watershed.

In 1875 the raja died. The Deputy Commissioner in Darjeeling pre-empted the court intrigue by causing the raja's brother and heir to be proclaimed ruler, a move in which Lhasa silently acquiesced. Sir Richard Temple, Lieutenant Governor of Bengal, made several tours of Sikkim, and during this period a road was constructed up to the Jelep La on the border between eastern Sikkim and Tibet

The British government always had an eye to developing trade with Tibet, and in 1883 Colman Macauly, Financial Secretary to the Government of Bengal, endeavoured to open trade routes up the Lachen valley to Tibet, the province of Tang being famous for producing good quality wool. He also tried to arrange free passage of Indian traders to Tibet and the easing of restrictions on trade through Sikkim and Darjeeling.

Complications set in, as the Chinese had recently annexed the north-east frontier of Upper Burma without there being a British response. The monastic authorities in Lhasa interpreted this as a sign of weakness, and adopted a much more aggressive attitude. In 1886 Tibetan troops advanced over the Jelep La, 30km into Sikkim, where they built a fort at Lingthu and blockaded the road.

The Raja of Sikkim, when pressured by the Lieutenant Governor in Darjeeling to ease restrictions on British subjects, declared that Sikkim was subject only to China and Tibet, and that he would need permission from the Tibetan government to visit Darjeeling. In 1886 he had signed a treaty acknowledging Sikkim's dependence on China and Tibet, promising to prevent British subjects crossing from West Bengal into Sikkim. Strong undercurrents had developed in Sikkim, born of a fear of Nepalese incursions from the south, and a profound dislike of the British on the part of the Tibetans. Caught between these two opposing forces, many people in Sikkim felt that the British could not offer practical protection, and that it would be wiser to turn to Tibet. Sikkim at that time could not be self-supporting, and should British support be withdrawn it would fall prey either to Tibet or the Nepalese warlords.

In 1887 the British Government wrote to the Tibetan commander at Lingthu, asking that they evacuate the position by 20th March, 1888, or force would be used. The Tibetans withdrew, and then re-invaded three times, until finally in 1888 General Graham advanced on the Tibetan position at Lingthu with orders to restore the *status quo*, but not to pursue the Tibetan force beyond the border. The lamas misinterpreted the movement and massed fresh forces along the crest of the Tukola Ridge. Sikh pioneers and a detachment of Gurkhas drove the Tibetans off the ridge, pursuing them over the Jelep La into the Chumbi valley.

The border position was formalised by an Anglo-Chinese convention, which was signed on 17th March 1890 by Lord Lansdowne and the Chinese Resident in Calcutta. This stated that 'The boundary of Sikkim and Tibet shall be the crest of the mountain range separating the waters flowing into the Sikkim Teesta (*sic*) and the affluents from the waters flowing into the Tibetan Mo Chu and northwards into the rivers of Tibet'. This established a British protectorate over Sikkim, but the Tibetans never formally recognised it and the Chinese were unable to impress them. Despite these obstacles, an agreed trading station was set up at Yatung in the south of the Chumbi valley.

The first mission house at Ringin (1899), with Miss Mathilda Johannson

Evening school students with Rev Gyampo Tshering and missionaries Siiri Aartola and Elin Kronqvist

In 1890 the legendary John Claude White was appointed as Political Officer and stationed in Gangtok In 1894 he was sent to Yatung to attend the opening of the market, and authorised the erection of a boundary pillar at the Jelep La, which the Tibetans promptly demolished.

During this period one sees the first real move to explore Sikkim since the pioneering journeys of Joseph Hooker. In 1884 a Frenchman, M. Robert, with Rinzin Namgyal crossed from Nepal into north-west Sikkim over the Jonsong La, and travelled down the Lhonak Chu to Lachen. Claude White with Hofmann travelled from Talung to Zemu, and then over the Thay La to the Lhonak valley in 1891, and in 1902 returned to the area to take a large party up the Langpo Chu to the pass of the Chorten Nyima La.

In 1899 Douglas Freshfield made his famous journey around Khangchendzonga. Travelling from Lachen, he reached the Zemu glacier, crossed over into the Lhonak valley and then north over the Jonsong La, before circling north of the mountain mass and down into east Nepal. He was also the first person since Hooker to make any plant collection from the region.

Around this time a series of disastrous military adventures by China had weakened its hold on Tibet. The Tibetans, who destested their Chinese overlords, and felt in no way bound by any agreements between the Chinese and British governments, started to create all manner of problems along the border with Sikkim, blocking trade, destroying boundary marks and making incursions into Sikkimese territory, where they claimed the land north of the Donkya La, Gyaogang and the Lhonak valley. At the same time the Russians were advancing their empire and influence eastwards, and through Tibet could easily threaten India's northern border. The Indian Mutiny was still a vivid memory, and the viceroy, Lord Curzon, felt that any disruption of British rule could act as a catalyst and provoke a similar disturbance.

Approaches were made on many occasions to the Chinese authorities in Lhasa, and to the Dalai Lama, to honour agreements and stop the border annoyance. Letters were returned unopened, and intelligence was received that the Tibetans had visited the Russian court at St. Petersburg, and were in close liasion with them, possibly negotiating a secret treaty. Finally, in 1903, the decision was made to send a military mission to Lhasa under Col Francis Younghusband.

Sir Tashi Namgyal, Claude White, the Royal Family and missionaries in Gangtok, 1920

The expedition left Darjeeling and journeyed up the Tista valley to Claude White's Residency at Gangtok, reaching Thanggu on 26th June. In his journal, Younghusband remarks on the abundant giant rhubarb (*Rheum nobile*) growing there. Capt O'Connor and Claude White pressed on to the pass north of Thanggu where the Tibetans had erected a wall, and there they were met by the Dzongpen of Khampa Dzong and two officials from Lhasa. The Tibetans appeared to have no authority to negotiate, so the British party pushed on to Gyaogang.

Younghusband, well aware that the Tibetan forces were building up ahead of him to prevent any further advance, ordered a halt at Khampa Dzong, which they fortified and patrolled. Meanwhile, Capt Walton was busy collecting specimens of birds for the British Museum, and Col Prain (later director of Kew) collected plants.

Khangchendzonga from north-east Nepal

Realising that progress north through Sikkim was unwise, Younghusband re-routed the main expedition over the Jelep La on 12th December into the Chumbi valley, but not without considerable problems with the animal transport. Eight thousand yaks had been drafted from Nepal, but these were decimated by disease, so the decision was made to use pack bullocks and ponies, only to have the bullocks smitten with foot and mouth disease and the ponies with rinderpest. Thus the expedition finally left Sikkim on its historic journey to Lhasa.

Right: Gangtok bazaar, c. 1938

Below: Tibetan goodwill mission, with Viceroy and Lady Linlithgow

A period of peace now ensued, and during the early part of the century a number of explorers and climbers visited Sikkim. Dr A.M. Kellas travelled to Lachen in 1907, went up the valley to the Zemu glacier, climbing extensively in the area, reaching the Zemu Gap and the Simvu saddle. In 1910 he crossed the Jonsong La from Lhonak and climbed Langpo Peak (6955m), and in 1912 he climbed Khangchengyao (6878m) by the north-east route from Dongthung.

Extensive botanical exploration in north-west Sikkim was undertaken by W.W. Smith and G.H. Cave in 1909. They then travelled up to the head of the Lhonak valley to the Jonsong La and visited Chorten Nyima La before returning, Smith coming back over the Lungnak La to Thanggu. During the years between 1929 and 1932 the German Khangchendzonga expedition led by Paul Bauer and the expedition led by Professor Dyhrenfurth were all active around the Zemu and Lhonak approaches to the peak. Legendary climbers such as Frank Smythe, Bill Tilman, Marco Pallis and Peter Oliver were all involved. In north-east Sikkim in 1933 G.B. Gourlay and J.B. Auden, approaching from Lachung, crossed the Sebu La in both directions. They reached 5000m on Khangchengyao before bad weather drove them back.

Not all the expeditions of the early 20th century were purely exploratory, botanical or mountaineering. Herbert Stevens, a member of the British Ornithologists' Club, mounted an expedition to collect bird specimens. In December 1930 he travelled along the old southern trade route, which ran via the Natu La to Lhasa, collecting at Lingtam, Jeluk and Nathang before returning to Kalimpong in April 1931. Among the more than fifty species he collected were griffon vulture, lammergeier, steppe eagle, red-footed falconet, ibis-bill, impeyan, satyr tragopan, parrot-bills, woodpeckers and many species of finches.

Col Reginald Cooke was stationed in Shillong, Assam, and made more than a dozen climbing trips to Sikkim, scaling Kabur (7375m) in 1935. The years before the Second World War produced a flurry of climbing activity. In 1935 Mrs Townend, Mrs Atkins and Miss Griffin repeated Hooker's 1849 journey in reverse. From Thanggu they travelled north to Khangchengyao, past the Gurudongmar Tso, and down the Donkya La to Yume Samdong. The latter was also visited in 1936 by Capt Sams as part of his work for the Survey of India. In the same year F. Spencer Chapman and Col R. Cooke visited the Zemu area, climbing Fluted Peak, Sphinx, and Pyramid Peak, before returning over the Lungnak La to Thanggu and Lachen. Herbarium material was collected by this expedition and deposited at the Royal Botanic Gardens, Kew, London. Col Cooke returned in 1937 with John (later Lord) Hunt and his wife, to climb around the Zemu glacier on the east side of Khangchendzonga. In this same pre-war period Eric Shipton climbed Khangchengyao. Frank Ludlow and George Sherriff, accompanied by George Taylor, travelled from Kalimpong through southern Sikkim on their way to Lhasa, and thence east to the Tsangpo valley.

In the period immediately prior to the 1939-45 World War, the British authorities were giving serious thought to the probability of attack by hostile forces into north-east India. Lt Ken Shepheard and Lt A.F.H. Jack, both of the Royal Engineers (Bengal Sappers and Miners), were dispatched from Darjeeling to survey possible routes for motor transport into Tibet.

They set out in a fleet of Baby Austin cars from Darjeeling, and then from Gangtok endeavoured to reach the Natu La. Road conditions were not conducive to little cars, and before many miles they had to resort to riding ponies, passing Tsango Lake and crossing the pass to reach Yatung. There they met a party comprising the political agent Sir Basil Gould, the Maharaja (Chogyal) of Sikkim and Raja Dorje of Bhutan. Shepheard comments in his diary: 'Gould is awe-inspiring but improves on contact, the Maharaja is a nice man but seems afraid of life, while Dorje is charming and interesting.'

From Yatung they rode on to Gyantse, where at the time the British Government

Baby Austins preparing to leave Darjeeling for Gangtok, August 7th, 1938

PICTURES FROM AN EXPEDITION

In 1938, with the British authorities concerned about attack by hostile forces in north-east India, Lt Ken Shepheard and Lt Archie Jack of the Royal Engineers were dispatched from Darjeeling to survey possible routes for motor transport into Tibet. Ken Shepheard's photographic record has survived, and a selection is reproduced here.

Above left: Pack horses at Gangtok rest-house

Above: Pulchoir Choide Gompa from Gyantse Dzong

Left: Ploughing fields below Gyantse Dzong

Above: The Tibetan Regent at the Potala

Right: Khud-side road slip near Gangtok

Below: The Potala, Lhasa

Below right: Chomolhari range seen across Rham Tso

Young Sikkimese men, c. 1940

maintained a garrison, and from there they planned to return. To their amazement they were given permission to proceed to Lhasa, where they were entertained most hospitably by senior officials and given an audience with the Regent – the present Dalai Lama having not been identified at that time. Even after more than sixty years the quality of Shepheard's photographs recording their journey (*pages 34–35*) is remarkable.

They returned uneventfully over the Jelep La, although Archie Jack, on his return to Gangtok, recounts a story of Bill Williams of the Survey of India, who was struck by lightning while in his tent in North Sikkim. He was badly burned and shocked, but his Indian assistant saved his life, transporting him back to Gangtok on a litter and thence to hospital in Darjeeling.

On their return Ken Shepheard left almost immediately for his regiment, but Archie Jack set off again on 16th October 1938, travelling north up the Tista through Bitu to Mangan. He then turned north-west up the Talung Chu, which he describes as 'difficult', and there the diary entries cease.

The war effectively put a stop to further climbing and exploration, although in 1944 Col Cooke made a attempt to climb Khangchengyao. Eleanor Bor and her husband Dr N.L. Bor (one-time assistant director of Kew and author of the 1953 *Manual of Indian Forest Botany*), drove from Assam to Gangtok. There they were entertained by Sir Basil Gould, and Maj

and Mrs George Sherriff, who had just returned from Lhasa. The Bors travelled up to Tsomgo Lake and over the Jelep La to Yatung in the Chumbi valley, where they took the opportunity to travel up the western slopes of Chomolhari. Eleanor Bor remarks that many tourists were passing through the area at that time.

The immediate post-war period saw another surge of activity. In 1945 William Noyce ascended Khangchengyao by the north-east face, a feat repeated in 1949 by Robert Walter. Col Cooke with Mr Morris and Ang Tharkay attempted Chombu in 1948, and in the same area John C. Templer, who lived for some time in Kalimpong and Darjeeling, travelled extensively in Sikkim making a geological study which included the area north of Yume Samdong.

T.H. Braham and M. Hruska made a remarkable journey in 1949. Starting from Lachung they climbed up to the Karpu La, and then descended the Jakthang Chu to Yume Samdong. From there they went north-east over the Donkya La and attempted to climb Khangchengyao from the north. They then went on to Dongthung, returning via Thanggu and Lachen. Fosco Marini with Prof Tucci's expedition to Lhasa returned over one of the Chola Range passes south-east of Lachung to Gangtok.

Tourism of a slightly less strenuous nature was also being promoted, and the booklet by Annie Perry (*Kalimpong and the Sikkim Hills* 1949) makes interesting reading. Airways (India) Ltd advertised flights from Calcutta to Bagdogra, which took 1hr 50min. One tour went from Kalimpong via Lingtam, Nathang (where the cemetery for casualties of the 1888 and 1904 army expeditions was situated) to the Jelep La and Natu La, returning via Gangtok along what was then a cart road. A second tour via Singtam and Temi visited the ancient monastery of Tashiding, where she describes the Bhum-Chu 'Water Pot' ceremony. A vessel full of water was sealed by a state official and deposited in the monastery. After one year the seal was broken and the level of the water in the pot was checked. A rise in the level portended good crops, while a fall was reckoned to be unlucky.

The third tour went west via Gangtok and Tung to Tsunthang, where one could stay in the government bungalow. It was still in good condition when I was there in 2001. She notes that in time past one trial by ordeal involved suspected criminals being dropped from the bridge just west of the town into the deep gorge of the Tista Chu. If they were drowned they were guilty, while if they emerged alive they were presumed innocent. One assumes that this kept the prison population at a suitably low level. From Tsunthang the route went to Lachen, with its hot springs at Samkhongmu and the headquarters of the Finnish Mission. The missionaries had introduced home industries there and in Lachung, which included weaving and apple culture, and founded a school in 1900. Early photographs show pioneer Miss Mathilda Johansson (*see page 29*) in front of the first mission house, near what is now Mangan, and Miss Siiri Aartola with Pastor Gompo Tshering at Lachung. The tourist route then passed north to Thanggu and Gyaogang, before turning east up the Chumbu Chu north of Khangchengyao and Gurudongmar. It returned south through Yume Samdong, Yumthang, Lachung and Gangtok.

Above: First school in Lachen, c. 1900

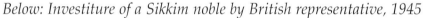
Below: Investiture of a Sikkim noble by British representative, 1945

Having covered much of this route in recent years, I am amazed at what was reckoned a tourist route, and have secretly wondered how many people ever travelled the whole way. Nowadays restrictions would prevent one repeating the journey.

In 1950 the Indo-Sikkim treaty was signed, when India assumed responsibilities for the defence of Sikkim, for external affairs and communications.

British tactics in the past had been to encourage large scale Nepalese immigration to Sikkim, the idea being that their affinity in matters of religion and culture would gradually wean Sikkim away from looking to Tibet for direction and support. The Indian government continued to encourage the Nepalese, who were now numerically superior to the ethnic Sikkimese, and at the same time implied that they were being treated as second-class citizens.

The Chogyal of Sikkim, Sir Tashi Namgyal, was a recluse, devoting his life to prayer and religious painting, so that much devolved to his son, Prince Palden Thondup Namgyal. He took a keen interest in initiating large scale development activities, and in setting up a modern administrative structure in the state, with the view of stimulating a more active role for Sikkim in the eastern Himalaya. This envisaged a greater degree of autonomy from India, whose protectorate Sikkim had become after the withdrawal of British influence in 1949, a concept which was viewed unfavourably by the Government of India.

The Chinese invasion of the North-east Frontier Agency in 1962 was a deep shock to the Indian Government, and led to a basic reappraisal of the strategic importance of Sikkim on India's northern border with Chinese-occupied Tibet. Thondup Namgyal was viewed with suspicion in some quarters, a situation not helped by rumour, false allegations and the mis-reporting of the royal couple's public speeches. A wild rumour circulated that Sikkim was planning a Himalayan Federation and revision of the Indo-Sikkim Treaty of 1950. The Indian media did not help by creating agitation among the Nepalese resident in Sikkim, and there was active encouragement of Kazi Lhendup Dorji, who was a defrocked monk of the Rumtek monastery, and well known as a political scourge of the ruling family. Dissident groups took part in well orchestrated 'popular demonstrations', and political tension built up to the point

Top: Rev. Gompo Tshering with Miss Siiri Aartola

Bottom: The Chogyal with local gentry, Gangtok Residency, 1940

Bottom right: Political group, 1953–54. Left to right, Mrs Pant, Crown Prince Palden Namgyal, Indira Gandhi, Pandit Jawaharlal Nehru, Chogyal Sir Tashi Namgyal and the Dewan, Nari Rustomji

where a referendum was forced on the Chogyal. Unification with India was steam-rollered through, and the Chogyal and his family ousted. After this, few western travellers were able to visit Sikkim.

For the next two decades all the climbing expeditions to north Sikkim were carried out by Indian climbers. In 1961 a large expedition led by Sonam Gyatso climbed Khangchengyao from the north, and Devi Singh, Pemba Gyaltzen and Nima Tsering made the first ascent of Chombu. In 1977 Lady Noel MacLehose was with a party who journeyed from Gangtok to Pemayangtse monastery. They then walked to Yuksam and on to Bakkhim, there being no road at that time. In 1979 Sonam Wangyal made the first ascent of Siniolchu, and in the early 1980s expeditions by Norbu Sherpa and Capt Negri, Maj Vijay Singh and Capt Sadshiva all climbed Khangchengyao by various routes.

It was not until 1983 that there was any further western participation, when Dr. Geoffrey Neuss led a party of young climbers north from Yuksam to the Goecha La and on to Kabur. They were followed only a few weeks later by the 1983 Alpine Garden Society Expedition, the first official botanical party since the travels of Smith and Cave. Their report on the expedition, a saga of wonderful plants and scenery – mixed with drama and hilarity in equal proportions – will strike a chord with anyone who has ventured into the Himalaya. On their very first day a huge case with all the scientific gear in it went missing between Delhi and Bagdogra. The contents were vitally important to their field work, and in due course the precious case caught up with them, carried by a relay of

porters. Himalayan porters are a race apart. I have seen one carrying a sofa on his back (not a small sofa either), and I have been passed at speed at 6000m by a porter carrying a load three times heavier than my own heavy pack. It is a chastening experience. On our 1996 trip we also suffered the loss of the biggest bag with all the scientific collecting gear, but in our case it never caught up with us until after our return to Britain.

The AGS party experienced foul weather much of the time, with thick mists or heavy rain – and, thanks to all the moisture, the forests were alive with leeches. In times past it was possible to travel to avoid the worst excesses of the monsoon, but recently it seems that the weather patterns have changed, and if you happen to experience fine weather you are fortunate. Storms such as that which hit us in Bhutan in 1985 have become more frequent and unpredictable, while the monsoon now seems to be edging into areas that have traditionally been regarded as dry.

The weaving industry was started in Lachen and Lachung from 1900–08

Palace of His Highness the Maharaja Sir Tashi Namgyal, October 1938

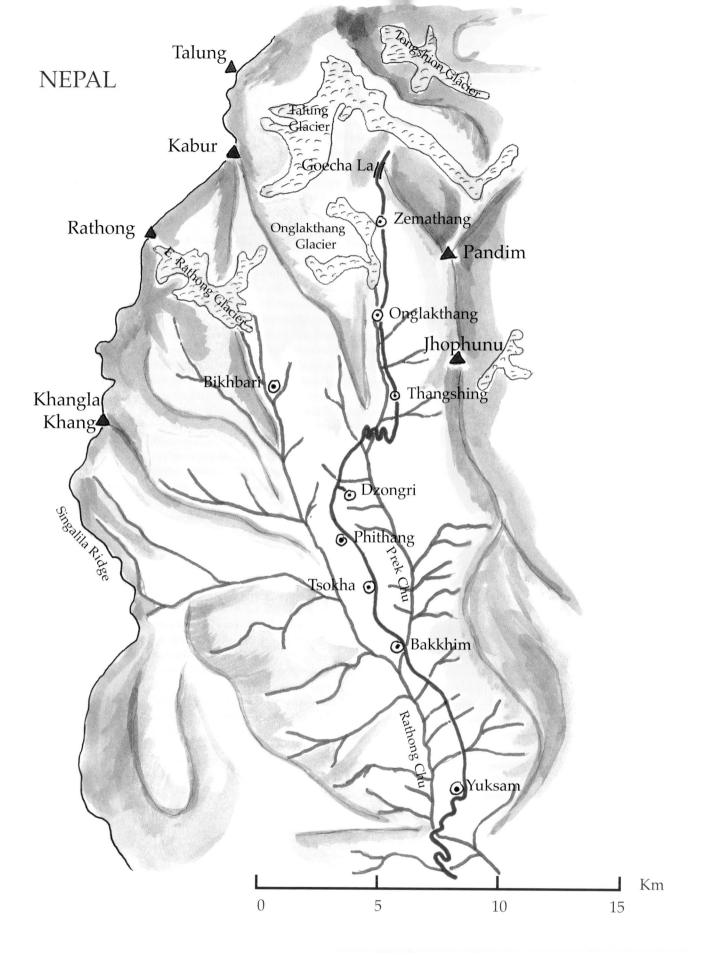

NEPAL

Talung

Kabur

Rathong

Khangla
Khang

Talung Glacier

Goecha La

Onglakthang
Glacier

E. Rathong Glacier

Singalila Ridge

Tongshion Glacier

Zemathang

Pandim

Onglakthang

Jhophunu

Bikhbari

Thangshing

Dzongri

Phithang

Prek Chu

Tsokha

Bakkhim

Rathong Chu

Yuksam

Km

0   5   10   15

The Delectable Mountains

Rhododendron barbatum

*O*ur faces were glued to the windows, to be rewarded by the view of Everest and Makalu towering above the clouds, with several other huge peaks away to the east . . .

Jhophunu and Kasture Ridge

Our flight with its dramatic views of Everest took us from Delhi to Bagdogra. It was April 1987, and I was leading a small trekking party to north-west Sikkim, following the route taken both by Dr Neuss's party and the Alpine Garden Society expedition of 1983.

Later we drove across the flat plain out of Siliguri, across the paddy fields dotted with snow white egrets, by telephone lines punctuated by perching brown-backed shrikes and black drongos with long forked tails. This time our road took us north, twisting and turning as it climbed towards Darjeeling. *Ageratum conyzoides* flowered in sheets of blue on the edges of the teak forest and the tea gardens, and everywhere bushes of pink and yellow flowered *Lantana camara* glowed in the sun. The hills became shrouded in mist as we climbed higher, the stream gullies full of the tall bushes of *Datura sauveolens*, the huge white trumpet flowers looking very sinister in the gloom. The grubby roadside shacks were covered in blue flowered *Ipomaea caerulescens* and the blue slogans of the Gorkha National Liberation Front, the latter declaiming the

rights of an independent Gorkhaland, for at that time there was considerable political unrest, with pressure from the GNLF for a separate Gurkha state.

At 1400m we emerged from cloud into sunshine at the village of Kurseong, and immediately became aware of birds everywhere – swifts, shrikes, crag martins, bulbuls and cuckoos. This area is famous for tea growing, the neatly trimmed low bushes spreading as far as we could see, interspersed with a few tall sal trees which act as shelter belts and give the workers welcome shade from the midday sun. Along the edges of the tea gardens we found masses of *Zephyranthes carinata* with flowers wide open like brilliant pink crocuses. Along with the *Lantana*, *Ipomaea* and *Datura*, they are all alien introductions to the Himalaya, where they are flourishing in the moist warm climate.

The other joy of the drive to Darjeeling is the light railway, which climbs over 5000m from the plains in a series of loops and curves unique in railway construction. The story goes that the engineer in charge of building the railway was sitting fiddling with one of his wife's curved hair-grips, while she completed her toilet. The grip was made of two curved combs connected by a hinge. Idly opening and shutting the grip, he suddenly realised that he had the solution to the problem of getting the railway line up to Darjeeling – build the track in a vertical zigzag of shallow curves. So steep is the climb that the little 040 Well Tank engines have to reverse up certain sections. They look as if they had been designed by Roland Emmett, the artist whose eccentric drawings once delighted readers of *Punch* magazine.

Darjeeling Light Railway

FLOWERS OF THE DARJEELING REGION

Above and below: Datura sauveolens and Zephyranthes carinata

Right, above and below: Rhododendron dalhousiae and Coelogyne nitida

Mother and child, Tibetan refugee centre

Mary Tenduf-la, owner of Hotel Windamere

There are no barriers across the road as it crosses and recrosses the railway line, so we were forced to drive with the windows down to listen for the imminent charge of a train out of the dense mist. The blue-liveried engines and rolling stock were built in late Victorian England by Kitson, and are now showing signs of their age. It is only the dedication of the engineers that keeps them going, and it will be a sad day when they cease to run. Further on we stopped to photograph our first rhododendron, *Rhododendron dalhousiae* with huge yellow flowers, the ground beneath the bushes studded with tiny blue annual gentians. On the rocks above grew the epiphytic orchid *Coelogyne nitida* covered in white blossoms with orange blotched lips.

Finally we reached Darjeeling, where we stayed in the fine Edwardian Windamere Hotel. The director, Mary Tenduf-la, was a keen gardener, and everywhere flowerbeds blazed with colour, and all the verandahs were packed with tubs full of flowering shrubs.

Mary was a tiny person, always immaculately dressed in Tibetan style. Rising every morning at 4am, she always looked the same, and I found myself wondering whether she ever slept. She ruled the Windamere with an iron hand, so that everything ran in a well ordered fashion. Hot water-bottles appeared like magic at bedtime, a very welcome comfort in the cold dampness of April nights in Darjeeling. At dinner the staff all wore white uniforms, each waiter topped with a white turban bearing his number. The dinner that night was a mite uninspiring, meat and two veg with blancmange to follow – just the sort of food Edwardian parents would have sent up to the nursery for the children. What followed later in the evening was perfectly in keeping. In the lounge a party of bird-watchers on a Himalayan tour sat around a splendid log fire, sorting out all the birds that they had seen during the day. Promptly at 10 o'clock an elderly and very small ayah appeared. Brooking no protest, she shooed them all off to bed. It was quite a sight to see a group of large, bearded, grown-up men being shepherded out by that tiny but determined figure. They certainly looked sheepish! Heavy rain drumming on the corrugated iron roof soon lulled me to sleep.

We awoke to thick mist and heavy showers of rain, with no sign of the mountains which lay out somewhere beyond the all-pervading greyness. Following the Chinese invasion of Tibet, many refugees have settled in West Bengal in and around Darjeeling, and we visited the Tibetan refugee centre to the north of the town. This was a hive of activity, and we watched craftsmen and women weaving, wood carving and painting. Visitors looking for carpets to buy would be well advised to spend time there, as the quality and traditional designs are excellent. I was curious to know what dyes they used in these carpets, expecting to be told of extracts of plant leaves and roots made to traditional recipes handed down from generation to generation. 'Oh, no,' they said, 'the German aniline dyes are far more reliable.'

In the centre I was delighted to see both Tibetan spaniels and Tibetan terriers as treasured family pets, as I am fond of both breeds. They looked in fine condition, well groomed, with leather collars studded with brass ornaments including little bells. I was amused to see one little terrier being washed in a mountain stream by its elderly owner – a picture of damp misery covered in soap suds.

Nearby, at the top of Darjeeling town, we passed the massive hoist system which delivers coal mined at Bijambri 8km away down in the valley, a unique way to get fuel into the town perched so high on its mountain ridge.

It is worthwhile to walk out to the edge of the town along the zigzag roads – there is always something interesting to see. We soon found some fascinating cobra lilies, so named for the hood-like spathe which covers the flower of these relatives of our own Lords-and-Ladies. *Arisaema propinquum* has a green hood striped with magenta, from which emerges an extraordinary threadlike appendage fully 45cm long which trails on the ground. *Arisaema tortuosum* is much taller, with a spadix spiralling up like the nose of Lewis Carroll's 'slithy tove' in *Through the Looking-Glass*. Up on the less accessible rock faces we found two fine orchids, *Coelogyne cristata* and *C.barbata* with a fringed lip bearing two bright orange ridges. Both *Rhododendron triflorum* and *r.maddenii* were in flower, and Hooker's name was remembered in *Viola hookeri*, which has white flowers veined with mauve.

Primula gambeliana flowered in every damp nook and cranny in and around Darjeeling, delicate little spires of pinky

The extravagant spiralling spadix of Arisaema tortuosum

45

purple flowers with yellow 'eyes'. In the treetops black-capped sibias and green-backed tits were singing, and I watched one sibia delicately drinking nectar from the waxy red flowers of the epiphyte *Agapetes serpens* high up in the fork of a tree. Himalayan siskins, firecrests and little pied flycatchers were busy flitting around in the fir trees, all within a stone's throw of the hotel. The bazaar in Darjeeling is an Aladdin's cave to delight western eyes. If you buy nothing else, ensure you purchase an umbrella, cheap and indispensable for any trekker. As a protection against rain, snow and falling leeches, you will not regret the expenditure of a few rupees.

To anyone addicted to tea, Darjeeling bazaar is a must. A wonderful array of different brands is on sale, and you can have a fine time testing them before you buy, rubbing the leaves between your hands to warm them and release their fragrance. Another necessity you should buy is ear-plugs. Himalayan dogs suffer from chronic

Above: Heavily laden porter in the Darjeeling bazaar

Right: Paris polyphylla

Below: Another view of the bazaar

insomnia, and in the towns and villages packs roam the streets fighting and barking into the small hours, at which time the local population awakes and takes on the task of denying you sleep. Even in the mountains the dogs bark endlessly, and in any case it is more than likely that one of your camping companions will snore.

Next morning we rose at 4am to make the obligatory journey to Tiger Hill to see the dawn come up over the mountains. I secretly felt that it scarcely warranted the loss of sleep. We had been advised not to waste too much time at the top of the hill, but descend to where an ornamental arch had been built across the road, and there walk into the forest along a well-marked track. This proved good advice, and we saw a wealth of birds including the stunningly coloured Mrs Gould's sunbird, gold-crowned black finch, blue-headed rock thrush and a delightfully tame yellow-bellied fantail flycatcher, which danced on a twig above our heads, flirting its black and white tail. The forest flowers were also fascinating, the one which most appealed to my companions being *Paris polyphylla*, each large flower bearing long filamentous purple petals.

The early start did mean that we were able to make a day trip to the orchid sanctuary at Takdah, where an effort is being made to conserve in cultivation as many native orchid species as possible. A visit in March or October is best, when many species will be in flower, but it is worthwhile coming at any time of the year, and the trip out from Darjeeling makes an enjoyable excursion.

We had scarcely set out when the view of Khangchendzonga and its attendant peaks, clear as crystal above the clouds 45km away, made us leap out of our landrover, cameras in hand.

All along the roadside we enjoyed the sight of birds and flowers we had not seen before, hoopoes, white-eyes, yellow-bellied warblers, red and black minivets, flycatchers of all sorts, with the bell-like call of the great Himalayan barbet ringing out over the valleys whenever we stopped to enjoy a particularly fine view. The barbet's call is loud and wild, and seems to embody the spirit of the forest.

By the roadside we found yet another cobra lily, *Arisaema ochracea*, and a fine colony of the little terrestrial orchid *Spiranthes sinensis*, with tiny pink and white flowers in a spirally wound spike.

Tiger Hill at dawn

Lamas playing rhakdong at the Yiga Chhoiling monastery

Inside the monastery

On our way back we visited the Yiga Chhoiling monastery of the Nyingmapa sect, founded in 1850 and the oldest monastery in Darjeeling. Set on a high ridge, it has superb views west to Khangchendzonga. The lamas brought out the 4m-long ceremonial trumpets called rhakdong, and blew them for us to hear. The sound can best be described as a huge, deep toned, musical fart. We were invited to try our luck at blowing them, which I just managed, to the amusement of the kindly lamas.

An early start saw us on the road to Sikkim in bright sunshine, driving out through the tea gardens of Pashok, with a fine view across the Tista valley to the hill station of Kalimpong, perched on a high ridge to the east. All along the route we passed plantations of cardamom, grown for its valuable spicy seeds. The low-growing bushes are planted in sheltered gullies beneath the forest trees, and in many places there were cunningly constructed irrigation systems of bamboo gutters to carry water to the bushes from nearby streams.

From Pashok the road descended by a series of steep zigzags to the confluence of the Tista Chu and the Rangit Chu. I was a little apprehensive to find that Gorkhali separatists had dug road blocks across the road. These we filled in with rocks and drove over them without interference, although the thought had crossed my mind that someone might be concealed above us on the hillside armed with a gun.

From the border with West Bengal and Sikkim the road followed the valley of the Rangit Chu, through terraced hillsides of paddy rice. Here, as the road started to climb up from the valley, we saw our first

Magnolia campbelli with thin white petals 12cm across, and the alder tree *Alnus nepalensis* along the riverside with branches festooned with long, dark brown catkins.

At the valley of Likship we met up with our trekking staff, led by Dharmey Tenzing, the youngest son of Tenzing Norgay of Everest fame. There were problems at the next checkpoint, and it became evident that we should have to take a police liasion officer along with us on the trek, something we had all hoped to avoid.

The road now became incredibly rough, and our jeeps crawled along in bottom gear over broken rock and mud for mile after mile. Fields of hill rice, maize and buck-wheat dominated the landscape, and the

Black eagle circling overhead, Yuksam

Tea pickers at Pashok

architecture of the farmhouses changed to resemble closely the flat-roofed houses I had seen in Bhutan. Everything looked much cleaner and neater. We came upon a broken-down jeep completely blocking the road, with eight punctures in an incredibly bald tyre, and no spare. In bucketing rain our staff tried to help, but eventually in desperation and growing darkness we had to manhandle it to the side of the road. Reaching Yuksam in darkness, we stumbled up a muddy path to a simple but clean dak bungalow. After an excellent supper, we went outside to find a clear, starlit night, with a collared pygmy owl calling monotonously in the woods above us.

Yuksam is a pleasant village at the head of an open cultivated valley, with good paths and abundant birdlife. All around the bungalow were drongos, black- and red-vented bulbuls, pied bushchats and pretty, green plumaged gold-fronted chloropsis. Overhead a pair of black eagles circled, pestered by two noisy offspring, and in the

The trail to Bakkhim

background came the ringing calls of the great Himalayan barbets. We set off along a forest track with the snow peak of Kabur Dome shining up ahead in a gap in the mountains.

The forest above Yuksam is very fine, and we soon recorded three new species of cobra lily, *Arisaema erubescens*, *A.tortuosum* and *A.propinquum*, and we found our first red flowered *Rhododendron barbatum*. The forest trees were covered in epiphytes, red flowered *Agapetes serpens*, *Gaultheria griffithiana* with masses of blue berries, and climbing figs of the sort beloved as pot plants in dentists' waiting-rooms, but here disappearing 20m up into the tree canopy, with stems as thick as your arm.

We stopped for lunch in a sunny clearing buzzing with insects and attracting an abundance of forest birds, among them Pallas's, grey-faced and large crowned warblers, grey-headed, orange-gorgetted and fantail flycatchers, Mrs Gould's sunbirds resplendent in red, yellow and purple feathers, black-capped sibias singing lustily and Himalayan cuckoos with their monotonous hoopoe-like calls.

Here too the leeches were active, dropping off the bushes with a soft plop, to land on our umbrellas and crawling onto our boots if we stopped off the track even for an instant. A close look at the bushes revealed them by the hundred, nasty little black jobs sitting on the leaves, their heads waving in the air as they sought out their next host for a blood meal. Leeches are capable of crawling through the lace holes of your boots, swelling up bloated with your blood, before falling off, leaving a cut which continues to bleed under the effect of the anti-coagulant contained in their saliva. They are incredibly

Black-capped sibia
[David Cottridge/Nature
Picture Library]

difficult to kill, like an indestructible rubber band, and they stick to your fingers if you try to pull them off.

We crossed the Prek Chu by a rickety wooden bridge, and started the long slog up to the rest house at Bakkhim. By the track flowered *Rhododendron griffithianum*, which has beautiful smooth, plum-coloured bark, big leaves and white flowers tinged with pink. High up in the trees we spotted clusters of the orchid *Cymbidium hookerianum*, green petalled with an orange lip. Yet another cobra lily was found, the bizarre *Arisaema griffithii*, a sinister looking plant with large brown striped flowers, each with huge ear-like flaps on either side of the hood. We soon became adept at rapid botanical photography. It always pays to be first in the queue to photograph a good plant, before the leeches become alerted to your presence and move in to the attack.

The Bakkhim rest house was a trifle primitive, with an unspeakably vile toilet.

Cymbidium hookerianum

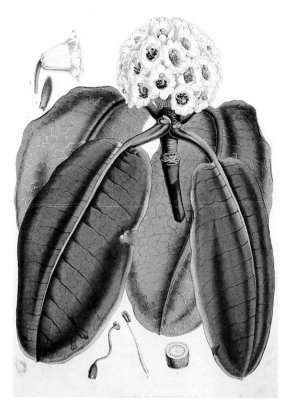

Rhododendron falconeri
Above: Hooker's drawing
[RGB Kew]

Above right: author's
photograph

Rhododendron lepidotum

The surly chowkidar responsible for keeping everything in good order had to be coerced to render it usable, otherwise it meant taking ones chances with the leeches behind a bush. One asset of the rest house was a huge dining table, around which we sat in the evening to sort out the plants and birds we had seen during the day.

Our police liasion officer was a most unhappy individual, ill equipped with a tiny knapsack, lacking both an anorak and a tent, and armed only with a kukri and a catapult. He trailed behind us, spurned by the porters who would not let him into their tents, so for the first few days he slept outside wrapped in a blanket. Finally he caught a diplomatic cold and was seen no more.

Next morning even the unspeakable loo was improved, and out of the window I saw a splendid Himalayan rubythroat and a flock of rufous-breasted accentors. We left Bakkhim, and plodded up the steep path in dense mist, everything dripping with moisture as we entered the rhododendron forest. Not only were the flowers beautiful, but the leaves of the different species showed a fascinating amount of variation. Rhododendron falconeri bore huge leaves with thick brown felt on their undersides and creamy flowers that were spotted with purple. R.dalhousiae had large creamy yellow flowers, while R.hodgsonii was pink and R.thomsonii had rounded smooth leaves. The branches twisted and interlocked so that the forest was dark, everything draped in dripping wet moss. Yet another cobra lily was found, *Arisaema nepenthoides*, the yellowish hood spotted and streaked with purple, as if it were suffering from several infectious diseases.

Lunch was taken under the shelter of a vast overhanging rock called Yomyom Puk – the moving rock. Despite the persistent drizzle, our cook Pasang got a fire going and conjured up a hot lunch with fresh roti. A little black puppy appeared as if from nowhere, and her mother turned up shortly afterwards. They accompanied us all the way up towards the Goecha La and back. Apparently they have followed every party of climbers or walkers who passed through Bakkhim.

The track now steepened, a long staircase of slippery logs and rocks through dense rhododendron forest, the banks beside the track covered in pink *Primula gracilipes*.

Camp was made at Phithang, where we were relieved to find the 'Rocket' toilet tent was already pitched, although it took the contortions of a Houdini to enter, and the zip did not work, necessitating the positioning of a strategic umbrella. The rain cleared, giving us wonderful views east to the sharp peak of Pandim and the jagged Jhopunu Ridge. Yellow flowered *Rhododendron wightii* was just coming into flower on the edge of the camp site, and we watched a pair of Nepalese sunbirds feeding on the flowers. That night was clear and cold, with the lights of Darjeeling visible in the far distance.

We woke to find that several centimetres of snow had fallen in the night. I walked into the forest before breakfast and watched Sikkim black tits and crested brown tits, which were extremely tame. We moved off through the mist, all the rhododendrons covered in snow, so that we were glad of our umbrellas to fend off great dollops which

Arisaema nepenthoides

Rhododendron wightii

Phithang after snow

53

Grandala

fell as we passed. The rhododendron forest was magnificent, composed for the most part of *Rhododendron arboreum, R.wightii, R.campbellii, R.thomsonii, R.falconeri* and the scarlet flowered *R.fulgens,* with blossoms so bright that they seemed to glow. As we emerged from the forest above the tree line the mountain slopes were carpeted with the dwarf rhododendron species, *R.niveum, R.lepidotum* and *R.anthopogon.* The leaves of the latter are covered in glands which secrete an aromatic oil, and they are gathered for burning as incense in the temples. I found the smell rather unpleasant, and walking through the bushes for a prolonged period can bring on a severe headache.

As we reached the top of the pass the sun came out briefly, and we had similarly brief views of a brightly coloured Impeyan pheasant, which took off like a rocket. The Impeyan or Monal is a big, bulky bird gorgeously coloured in green, bronze, blue and fawn, with a crown of shiny green feathers on top of the head.

We reached Dzongri at lunchtime, to find a stoutly built wooden bungalow set by a stream in a shallow valley full of dwarf rhododendrons. The ground was carpeted with primulas still tightly in bud, and the huge leaf rosettes of *Meconopsis discigera,* the leaves glistening with golden hairs. A party of snow-plastered German trekkers arrived, having failed to reach the Goecha La because of snow and thick fog. We all walked out to the surrounding hills, but it was difficult to see much in the murk, although I did surprise a solitary snipe in wet ground, a flock of brilliant blue thrush-sized grandala, and a single golden bush-robin, resplendent in black and gold.

Pasang dished up another superb meal at suppertime, and we retired to our sleeping bags on the floor of the hut as a few snowflakes fell outside and lightning flashed in the sky to the south over Darjeeling.

The next day started dry, the mountains and hills just visible in the mist, and we set off to walk to Thangshing. The path climbs up above Dzongri, before meandering across a hillside covered with dwarf rhododendrons, primulas and blue poppies. Eastwards the spire of Pandim was clear above the clouds which filled the deep valley below. It started to snow, and we slipped and slithered down the long steep descent to the Prek Chu. Under the bushes we found the dead flowering spike of *Xylanche himalaica,* a strange broomrape-like plant which is parasitic on the roots of rhododendrons.

Mid-morning the sun came out, and everything sparkled. One of the porters was waiting by the track with a brew of tea, which was most welcome, as several of us had severe headaches brought on by the altitude. As I put my rucksack back on, I dropped my camera down a deep hole in a rock fall. I could just see the strap nearly 3m down, and with a sinking heart wondered if I could ever manage to rescue it. The prospect of a trek without a camera was too awful to contemplate. I had reckoned without our resourceful porters, led by the charming and imperturbable Karma. They levered boulders about as if they weighed nothing, and with a bent branch fished out the precious camera. Oh, blessed porters!

Thangshing is situated in a small flat valley bounded on all sides by very steep slopes, with the spire of Pandim at the valley head. Soon after we arrived the weather closed in, with continuous sleet and hail. Memories of the disaster camp at Lingshi in Bhutan came flooding back, and there was a familiar sinister look to the sky, with long wisps of grey cloud.

Dharmey and I discussed the wisdom of moving up to Zemathang, since the camp at Thangshing had a stoutly built stone hut, while Zemathang was exposed, with no decent shelter for the porters. At 4pm there was a heavy hailstorm and the wind veered to the south-west. We decided on an early supper, built up a good fire in the hut, and cheered ourselves by singing silly songs, assisted by a tot of Shangri-la Sikkim whisky, thoughtfully supplied by Mrs Tenzing. The AGS Expedition had had similarly good reason to bless Mrs Tenzing!

At sunset, while sitting in the 'Rocket' contemplating Pandim lit by the evening sun, I watched a golden eagle and a shikra falcon circling against a backdrop of

Thangshing valley with Pandim

Young yak herder at Zemathang

Thangshing in snow

sparkling fresh snow. We arose the next morning at six, to find 5cm of snow lying, with snow still falling heavily. The decision was made to stay camped at Thangshing, so we walked some way up towards Zemathang, where we found a young lad of fifteen years old camping alone, looking after thirty-six yaks. He had come up early in April and would return to the valleys in October, his only company a transistor radio belting out Chinese pop music. The weather was now so vile that there was nothing to do but shelter, eat the splendid supper Pasang had made for us and lower the level in the bottle of Shangri-la.

I awoke at 4.30am to find our camp deep in snow, with the pole of my own tent badly buckled under its weight. Snow was falling heavily, so Dharmey and I decided to evacuate immediately and make for Dzongri, as there was a grave danger of being trapped in the Thangshing valley. We packed flasks of hot tea and left in haste, ploughing down through deep snow which had obliterated all trace of the track to the bridge over the Prek Chu, which we reached in two hours. The zigzag path up to the ridge beyond was desperately hard work, the snow over a metre deep, with snow laden trees and bushes collapsed across the track.

Brief clearances of blue sky illuminated a fairy tale world of sparkling white, with the great peaks all around trailing plumes of white. Even the river had disappeared under the snow, the boulders topped with so much of it that they appeared like a field of gigantic mushrooms.

We reached the top after several hours, and slogged on to reach Dzongri, where everyone flopped into sleeping bags to rest and warm up before we had some food. Several of our porters were snowblind, one had a bad cough and another had an infected cut leg, so I had quite a busy surgery and was thankful that we had beaten a retreat from Thangshing. At least from Dzongri it was mostly downhill to Yuksam.

A herd of yaks came down the track past the camp, where one poked its head into the loo tent which was occupied at the time. We could hear some fearsome oaths as the sitter beat it off with the umbrella. Another was stampeded by the yak man up the steps of the hut and into our room, where it pranced about, miraculously avoiding all our sleeping bags and gear. We were all laughing so much that we were precious little help in driving it out.

We got up at 6am to find a glorious sunny morning, so after a quick cup of tea we all climbed up the ridge to the north-east of Dzongri. The view that greeted us as we rounded the corner was fantastic. From Kokthang in the west, the entire mountain range lay before us, with Khangchendzonga towering in front of us. Freyr Peak, Rathong, Kabur, Kabur Dome and Talung glistened against a bright blue sky. East of Khangchendzonga a slope dropped away down to the deep valley where we could see our recent campsite at Thangshing. The valley side then rose equally steeply to the spire of Pandim, then eastwards to Jhopunu and the Kasture Ridge, with the sharp peak of Siniolchu just peering over the top. To the south it was clear to Tiger Hill and the Darjeeling ridge, and in between we could see Pemayangtse monastery gleaming in the sun. On my return to England I found that this was the very spot from which Joseph Hooker had drawn the view, and described it in lyrical terms.

While we sat and drank in the view, a lone helicopter flew over high on its way to

Pandim under snow

the Himalayan Mountaineering Institute base camp at Bikhbari, where an Indian expedition was trying to climb Rathong. Karma told me that at that time Pandim was still unclimbed. The problem was a vast collar of ice, which one could clearly see all round just below the summit, like the out-turned ribs of a gigantic umbrella.

Very soon the weather closed in again, and we retreated to the bungalow in thick mist and driving snow. Nearby was a small hut owned by the Forestry Department, where three young Sikkimese trekkers were sheltering. They had brewed some chang, and hospitably invited us down to share it. All my party were suffering to some degree, either from headaches, coughs or upset stomachs, so I went down on my own for a highly convivial evening, which was to have a lasting influence on my further adventures in Sikkim. Wangyal Tobden was an officer in the Sikkim police, broad shouldered and extremely fit. Lekshed Gyaltshen, tall and quietly spoken, worked in the planning department of the Government of Sikkim. Rajesh Lakhotia,

Jhophunu and Kasture Ridge before the weather closed in

small and very dynamic, was director of the Hotel Tashi Delek in Gangtok, where we were due to spend the final days of our holiday. They had been close friends from their school days and when the chance offered liked to trek together in the wilder parts of Sikkim.

They proved wonderfully entertaining company, and we spent a long time discussing the problems Sikkim faced in conserving its flora and wildlife, while at the same time opening itself up to tourists such as my own group. They were full of information about the local wildlife. In the early winter bharal (blue sheep - *Pseudonis nayaur*) come down to the lake at Thangshing, where a flock of Marco Polo sheep, (the eastern race *Ovis ammon* ssp.*hodgsonii*), have also been seen. Markhor have not been recorded locally, but for the last three years a very large, lone tiger, apparently of the Siberian race, had been seen regularly around Dzongri at the turn of the year. Local wildlife experts were certain that it was not of the forest race normally seen in Sikkim.

My friends had with them a young Lepcha yak herder as guide and helper. He was persuaded to tell me of a type of yeti, which he claimed to have seen regularly between Dzongri and Tsokha. The local name for it is Megyoi, or Ban Jagri in Nepali – literally 'wild witchdoctor'. He described it as 1–1.5m tall, having the same coloured features as a man, with shortish hair concealing the ears, and no beard. The feet were bare, and it walked upright like a man, not like a monkey. The local people say that it eats grubs and drinks a milky secretion from the back of a species of toad. He claimed that only certain people, such as

holy men, could see the yeti, but in all likelihood this is just a reflection on the fact that they sit quietly in contemplation, creating no disturbance. It is unwise to dismiss such stories out of hand. I have never seen a bear in the eastern Himalaya, but I have frequently seen evidence of their presence. Bears are relatively common, but any trekking party like ours makes so much noise that any self-respecting bear would be over the next ridge and out of sight. A creature such as that described by the yak boy would be even more likely to keep out of the way of the human species.

The author with Karma in front of Khangchendzonga

Bharal

Above: White-collared blackbird at Tsokha

Below: Plain-backed mountain thrush

I was full of enthusiasm for what I had already seen of north-west Sikkim. My friends told me that I should try to get permission to visit the northern region around Muguthang and the Lhonak valley, which they described as utterly remote and fascinating. If I were to get permission, they would make every effort to come with me. Little did they know what they were letting themselves in for!

Back some time later in the bungalow, I found that I had been turned out of my room to accommodate the local carpenter and his merry men, who were making chairs and tables for the hut. Dharmey and Pasang warned me that he was a thoroughly violent and unpleasant individual, and insisted that unless I moved in with them and the porters, the carpenter would make life miserable for everybody. I didn't mind in the least, as they had the stove in their room and it was distinctly warmer.

Overnight yet more snow had fallen, and it was still falling steadily. Several members of our party were feeling unwell, and the porters' food supplies were running short, so Dharmey and I discussed the possibility of moving down, first to Tsokha and then to Bakkhim as soon as we felt we could make it. By midday the weather was worsening in the manner all too familiar to me, and everyone was feeling poorly, so we decided to move straight down while we could. In heavy snowfall we ploughed down the trail to Tsokha. As we entered the rhododendron forest again we saw another Impeyan pheasant, feathered topknot and all, before it vanished in the gloom. Tsokha is pleasantly sited on an open ridge, where a new wooden tourist bungalow had just been completed, with a verandah facing south over the Rathong Chu valley. Here at 3500m there was no snow, and the sun shone.

The forest around Tsokha is full of birds and rich in flowers. Within a few minutes' walk of the bungalow we soon recorded more than 45 bird species, of which the most colourful were Nepalese and fire-tailed sunbirds, maroon oriole, white-browed rosefinch, fire-tailed myzornis, and the laughing thrushes – white-spotted, red-headed and black-faced. They appeared in family parties, playing follow-my-leader through the undergrowth, the black-faced laughing thrushes calling like cats mewing. Most exciting of all were a pair of black-browed parrotbills, small chunky birds with yellow beaks and black foreheads, which were busy pecking away at bamboo shoots.

Most of us had recovered considerably in the warmth and lower altitude, but Karma was felling unwell with congested lungs and a bad cough which required treatment. We walked out along the old track towards Bikhbari, which runs along the ridge well below the track by which we had descended from Dzongri. It proved a good choice, if a trifle narrow and slippery, leading to an open area of grazing land called Gunza.

There we added fulvous-breasted wood-pecker, Nepal treecreeper and nutcracker to our bird list. The delicate epiphytic *Rhododendron pendulum* was plentiful, growing on the branches of the larger rhododendrons, and I found a single clump of a *Cypripedium* orchid in leaf.

Pasang served us yet another excellent supper, and we retired happily into our sleeping bags, with heavy rain drumming on the roof of the bungalow. Sleep proved elusive. In the middle of the night a bunch of drunken travellers turned up and moved into the room next to mine, where they made so much noise that I was reduced to bellowing at them in such basic Gorkhali as I could remember, and thumping on the wall. Further excitement was provided by mice running over the girls' sleeping bags, their screams bringing Dharmey to the rescue.

Next morning we looked round the village, where the local farmers were busy threshing the crop of hill rice. Our cook Pasang borrowed a flail to demonstrate to us just how it ought to be done, and much to

Rhododendron pendulum

Tsokha with chortens

his chagrin broke it first wallop! The farmer's expression became even more resigned than before. In the morning sunshine the birds around Tsokha village were a delight, alpine swifts soaring against a backdrop of the snow peak of Pandim, and a tree full of yellow-browed and Pallas's warblers, orange-gorgetted fly-catchers, Nepal sunbirds, stripe-throated and rufous-vented yuhinas, all busy picking small insects from the moss covered tree trunks.

Right: Pasang threshing

Below: Forest track, Bakkhim

When we walked down to Bakkhim we found the villagers in a state of high excitement, as a bear with a cub had been seen. Unfortunately for us they had made so much noise that the bears had disappeared. Many plants had come into flower in the few days we had been higher up in the mountains, and by the track we found the tiny green epiphytic orchid *Liparis pusilla* and the lovely white and orange orchids *Coelogyne cristata* and *C.corymbosa*, the latter easily the prettiest member of the genus, with smaller flowers in elegant drooping sprays.

Our guide spotted a troop of langur monkeys, and by dint of climbing up a tree I managed to get a tele-photo shot of a big male sitting solemnly

on lookout, his long tail dangling down. When I got down I found the porters literally rolling on the ground in paroxysms of mirth. Eventually one choked out 'Oh, Sahib! One monkey up tree take picture of other monkey!' Golden-throated barbets were calling loudly in the treetops, gorgeous birds with green bodies and gold and orange heads with a black eyestripe. Their call - a ringing 'Quowp!' - can be heard at a great distance in the forest. Another bird, the grey-headed flycatcher, had a call that sounded like 'Khati bhaje?' in Gorkhali, so we christened it the Get Up Bird, as it was always saying 'What time? What time?'

Fully recovered from our adventures, we decided next day to hire a jeep and visit the famous monastery of Pemayangtse. Eventually we found one in what looked like reasonable condition, and agreed a price, although it meant taking the driver's mother, who owned the jeep, and her younger son. A formidable old lady, she promptly settled in the back seat like Queen Victoria in a state coach, and we set off. Shortly afterwards the silencer fell off, and we staggered along making a thunderous din. At Rimbi power station the driver stopped, and proceeded to dismantle the entire exhaust system, which he then started to weld together using tools belonging to the station engineers. I soon suspected that it had been his intention to do this all along, and that we had merely been conned into paying for the journey. After one and a half hours there seemed to be no prospect of continuing our journey, so I summoned both the driver and the owner and informed them that the next day in Gangtok I should report their conduct to my police friends. We then gathered all our gear, and set off with the apparent intention of walking all the way back to Yuksam. Soon afterwards we heard running footsteps, and turned to find the driver, very contrite and apologetic. With great difficulty I kept a straight face and demanded some of our payment back in reparation. Fortunately, good humour was quickly restored all round, and we finally set off to Pemayangtse.

The monastery was founded about 400 years ago by Gyalwa Lhatsun Chempo. I did not find it a particularly inspiring place, possibly because everything was shrouded in thick mist. The finest thing inside was a superb sangtrolpalri, an incredibly intricate tiered representation of the different levels of the Buddhist heaven and hell, with thousands of little figures of gods, demons, men and animals. This was the work of a single monk, and it had taken him all of seven years to complete.

Orange-gorgetted flycatcher

Male langur monkey, taken by 'another monkey'

Doorway,
Pemayangtse monastery

Tashiding gompa

Rangit Chu from Tashiding

Dharmey Tenzing and Mrs Daku
Tenzing

That evening in Yuksam we were joined by Mrs Daku Tenzing, who had arrived with a welcome supply of beer and rakshi. Pasang excelled himself, producing a memorable supper, and it was a very contented party that retired to bed. In the woods above the bungalow a spotted scops owl called mournfully.

I awoke next morning early to the sound of a pair of mynahs bouncing around on the tin roof of the bungalow. Not only did they squawk loudly, but this pair seemed to be wearing hob-nailed boots. The drive by jeep to Gangtok took us from Yuksam past the monastery of Tashiding, built high up on a ridge above the road. The track up is a steep but rewarding walk, with beautiful views over the deep Rangit Chu valley, and trees full of orchids. There were some particularly fine *Dendrobium densiflorum* with huge spikes of golden-yellow flowers. A cheerful farmer passed us carrying a load of green leaves as fodder for his animals, the load almost enveloping him, so that he resembled a bush on legs.

Tashiding was founded in 1717 by Ngadak Sempa Chenpu of the Nyingmapa sect. A series of graceful, well-proportioned buildings stretch along the wooded ridge, the carved wooden porch and doors of the main temple being particularly fine. Hooker visited Tashiding in 1849 and remarked on the huge 'funeral cypress . . called Tchenden by the Lepchas, Bhoteeas and Tibetans'. *Cupressus himalaica* is now known to be native to Bhutan, and the expedition to west Sikkim in 1992 by the Royal Botanic Garden Edinburgh found it at Dubde and Norbugang near Yuksam, exactly as described by Hooker. He also remarked, 'Beyond the temples are the chaits and

Tashiding gompa

mendongs . . . extremely picturesque, and those at Tassiding (*sic*), from their number, variety and size, their commanding and romantic position . . . are particularly so.' Tashiding had a serenity which was for me noticeably absent from the monastery at Pemayangtse, and from Rumtek which we visited later on. The buildings may have lacked the smartness of the newer gompas, but they had the sort of ambience which you find in a great cathedral, or some remote and simple little country church. An old lady, clad in a yellow shawl, bent and with a face wrinkled as a prune, was quietly circling the hilltop, silver prayer wheel spinning in her hand. She was there when we arrived and was still there

Chaits at Tashiding as photographed by the author and drawn by Joseph Hooker [RGB Kew}

as we left, and seemed to embody the spirit of Tashiding.

We had been accompanied from Yuksam by a forestry officer, anxious to get to Gangtok, and he now guided us down a steep track from the monastery to where our jeeps were supposed to meet us. The forest trees carried a rich flora of epiphytic orchids, more yellow *Dendrobium densiflorum*, pale mauve *D.aphyllum* and another dark purple flowered dendrobium too high up in the trees for us to identify. The forest trees were magnificent, with an understorey of *Sambucus adnata* like our own British elderberry, but with red berries, *Englehardia spicata*, *Albizia chinensis*, *Corylus ferox* and the alder *Alnus nepalensis*, over which scrambled the large yellow dodder *Cuscuta reflexa*. The forestry officer was an excellent guide to the trees but managed to lose us comprehensively, so our poor local guide, who had deferred to him as a senior officer, was flustered and sweating profusely by the time we found our jeeps. Several cold beers

at the village of Likship restored everyone to good humour for the drive down the river Tista to Singtam, where we turned north on the long winding climb up to Gangtok.

The Tashi Delek Hotel where we stayed in the Mahatma Gandhi Marg is built up above the Lal Bazaar, and proved most comfortable and well run. We had already met the director, Rajesh Lakhotia, at Yuksam, and we were well looked after. Local laws in Gangtok strictly limit the height of buildings to three storeys, in deference to the risk of earthquake, but a quick glance around served to confirm my suspicions that the law is more commonly observed in the breach. Buildings of seven and even nine storeys sprouted everywhere on the steep hillsides. Next morning we breakfasted in sunshine on the hotel roof garden, and watched the sparkling white peaks of Khangchendzonga away to the west, until the clouds rolled up from the valley and blotted out the view.

Gangtok has grown enormously in recent years, every available piece of ground which is not completely vertical being built upon, so the road system consists of a network of extremely steep zigzags. The Lal Bazaar was reached from the hotel by a long, slippery set of stone steps. A densely packed mass of covered stalls with brightly coloured umbrellas filled all the space between the houses, while those too poor to rent a stall laid out their wares on sacks and polythene sheets at the edge of the market. Here you could buy fruit and vegetables of a bewildering variety: potatoes, carrots, cabbages, tomatoes, plums, apples, mangoes, bananas, beans and okra, with other fruits and vegetables of unusual

colours and weird shapes, some covered in warts and spines. Most impressive were red and black radishes as big as parsnips. These tend to feature prominently in stews served up by trek cooks, and really are rather good.

Several stalls were selling curd cheese in slabs wrapped in banana leaves, and dried squares of yak cheese pierced with a hole to thread a string. These are carried by the locals on long mountain journeys, and sucked rather as we would suck a sweet to stop the mouth drying out at high altitude. I could never fancy them. They looked rather grey and well handled. Another stall, manned by a jolly rogue of a Bangladeshi, had dozens of highly coloured pots and tins full of spices and herbs. There was a stall selling farmed freshwater fish brought up by road from Bangladesh, and another

Gangtok from the Tashi Delek Hotel

Lal bazaar, Gangtok

had wicker baskets full of miserable scrawny chickens. Great barrels full of sinister looking dried fish, certain death to western stomachs, with an aroma you could hang your hat on, sat alongside chunks of crumbling dark molasses covered in flies. In one of the alleys between the market stalls a group of tailors was busy, bending over pedal-operated sewing machines. They would make you a shirt, trousers or dress literally while you waited. Behind them were the stalls which seem common to every market place throughout the world,

selling everything from pots and pans to plastic beads.

The people thronging the market were equally fascinating, Tibetan housewives with neat striped aprons, necklaces and ear-rings of lapis lazuli and coral, chubby round-faced Bangladeshi pedlars, dapper Nepalis with forage caps tilted at a rakish angle, shy Lepcha with bundles of herbs and dried mushrooms, while staggering between them hurried heavily laden porters with big conical bamboo baskets on their backs. For my daughter I particularly wanted

*Below and facing page:
Rumtek monastery, Gangtok*

to find some beads made of a special type of fossil coral, which gives them a wonderful cream and brown pattern. I soon found that the genuine beads were extremely expensive, and often used as part of a bride's dowry. They take hours to make, as the stone is very hard and difficult to drill through. However, imitation beads were available, if only I could find them with my limited vocabulary of Gurkhali. At one stall where I enquired, the owner insisted on coming with me to help in the search, leaving the stall in the capable hands of his wife. In perfect English, which put me to shame, he explained that the imitation beads varied greatly in quality, but eventually we did find some which he declared satisfactory. He would accept no recompense for his trouble, saying 'You are a guest in my country and are welcome!'

Sunday morning is the best time to visit the Lal Bazaar. All the world and his wife are there, rain or shine, and it constantly amazes me to see immaculate, sari-clad ladies picking their way between the mud and puddles, seeming quite unsplashable.

All too soon our time in Sikkim came to an end, but my Sikkimese friends had excited my curiosity to visit the north of the country. Nobody seemed to know anything about it, and its very remoteness rendered it all the more attractive.

Once home in England I set about reading every scrap I could find about Sikkim, but, like the maps of the region, it was not only out of date but woefully lacking in detail.

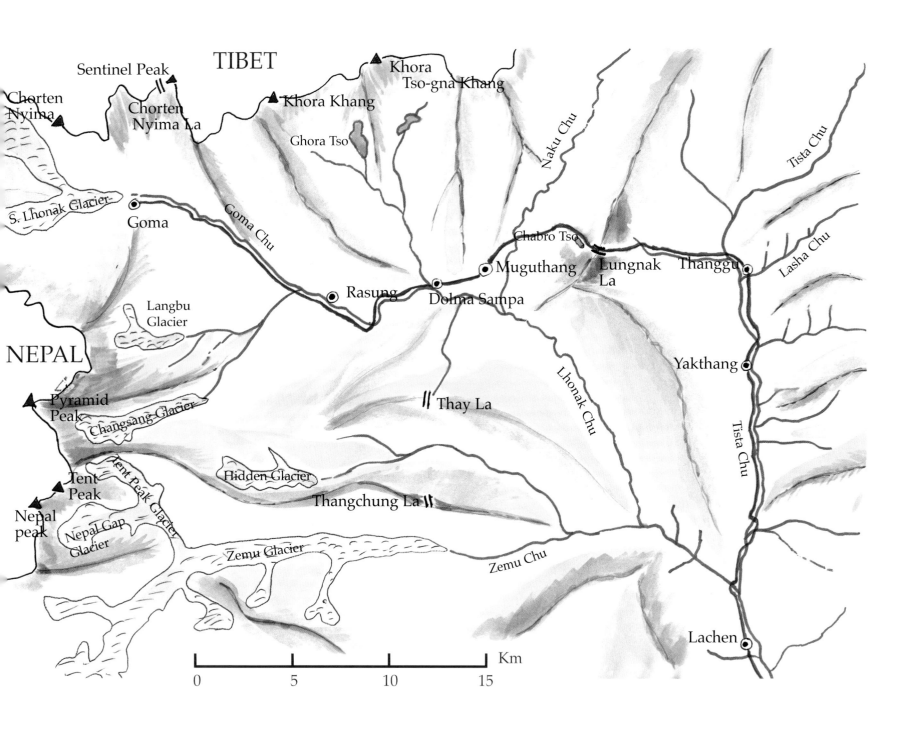

Against the Odds

Common mynah

Near Siliguri

*T*he possibility of returning to Sikkim hovered at the back of my mind. I was therefore delighted to receive a short treatise on yaks . . .

Top: Yak and calf

Bottom: Yaks in harness

Back home I was once more plunged into the hurly-burly of veterinary practice, although the possibility of returning to Sikkim hovered at the back of my mind. I was therefore delighted to receive a copy of a short treatise on yaks written by

Tshewang Rinzen, the redoubtable Dungpa of Lingshi, who had played such an active part in the helicopter rescue of our party from north-west Bhutan in 1985.

Tshewang Rinzen's letter rekindled my determination to return to Sikkim. He had trained as a veterinary officer, and worked in that capacity at Lingshi before taking up the more exalted post of Dungpa. I found his treatise fascinating, despite some curious English – but then I wondered what my own efforts would have been like if I had attempted to write in Dzonka or even in Gurkhali!

I hope that he will forgive me for quoting from his preface: 'Even though we gave lovely names to our animals to indicate the extreme regards and love we had for them, in fact I would like to vomit my local experience in Yak's management . . .'

Even when I met him in his official government capacity, his love of animals and farming had been obvious, and it did not surprise me when he retired to set up a chicken farm. His treatise was full of good, practical advice to yak farmers on the selection of breeds suitable for the area in which they lived, whether they were concentrating on milk production, or producing meat or wool.

The wild yak *Bos grunniens* is now a great rarity, with a few remaining in western Tibet. Nearly all the yaks one sees are domesticated, although they give the impression of being otherwise. A bull yak can weigh 600kg, standing over 1.8m at the shoulder, and equipped with an impressive spread of very sharp horns. The face is very long, with a lugubrious expression. Every part is clad in long hair, which drapes down the sides like skirts and finishes with a tail like a large feather duster. If you see the tail held vertically upwards and shaken, it is time to walk delicately, like the Biblical Agag – and to put a respectable distance between you and the yak.

The low-set eyes of the yak are in marked contrast to those of the buffalo, which appear to be set high in the skull, giving the impression that the beast is gazing upwards. A children's story told widely in the eastern Himalaya relates how the yak and the buffalo were cousins, and lived together in the valley where they shared a fur coat between them. One day the yak decided to set off for the mountains, and persuaded his cousin to lend him the precious fur coat for the journey. When he reached the mountains, he enjoyed it so much that he never came back, and evermore the buffalo looks longingly up to the peaks where his cousin – the yak – looks superciliously down.

The story also led to a joke on the relative merits of buffalo and yak meat, yak being

Pack yaks in the mountains

considered far more tasty. When given a plate of unidentifiable 'beef', the diner asks: 'Is this looking-up yak or looking-down yak?'

Three main breeds are recorded. Lho-gyag are the largest, being found only in Sikkim and the Chumbi valley. Bod-gyag are smaller, and there is a polled breed called A-yu. Colours vary from black to pale dun, with various mixtures of white. Black yaks with white tails are particularly highly valued.

Yaks can carry loads up to a height of 6000m and can cope with fairly deep snow. The feet are large, with big flexible hooves, so that when you are fording a river on yak-back you can sense the yak feeling carefully between the slippery rocks to get the best footing. I have a great respect for yaks.

When riding, steering is effected by means of a single rope attached to a ring in the nose. This feature, accompanied by iron stirrups far too short for lanky western legs,

The hybrid between the male yak and cow, or cow buffalo, is known as a dzo, or dzo-mu if female. There are many other local dialect names for them. They are far more tractable than pure-bred yak, being used as riding and draught animals. They do not carry such a thick coat, and therefore cannot work at such high altitudes as yak.

DZO

(To be sung to the tune of 'Down Below')

If you've gone and lost your way
    Ask a dzo.
If you're tired and feeling grey
    Ask a dzo.
They are patient, they are wise,
They've long lashes round their eyes,
And a little cloud of flies,
    Round a dzo.

If you've got a mound of tack,
    Use a dzo,
For they never answer back -
    That's a dzo!
If you're seated on the loo
And a dzo should join you too,
You need only mutter 'Boo!'
    At the dzo.

You could travel half the world
    With a dzo.
It is worth its weight in gold,
    Is a dzo.
Butter, milk and meat and hair,
All the things you need are there,
So go out and buy a pair.
    Have *two* dzo!

A finely caparisoned dzo

renders your ultimate direction a thing of chance. I never found a yak sensitive to heel pressure to go left or right, and where the brakes were remained a mystery. At walking pace the yak is a most comfortable ride. They can , however, move very fast with a curious loping gallop, which, coupled with the high wooden saddles and short stirrups, makes the experience the nearest thing to bloodless castration one is likely to encounter. Although yaks are capable of work at high altitude, they cannot adapt to low altitude, and the yak men dislike bringing them below 3000m. Below that height they are at high risk of developing acute pasteurella pneumonia, and also suffer from an unpleasant fungal skin disease.

Yak calves are the most charming animals, incredibly furry and bright eyed. It is my, as yet unfulfilled, desire to deliver a yak calf, but so far I have always been in Sikkim at the wrong time for the calving season. Yaks calve from early April to the end of August, the cows calving down for the first time aged two to three years. Thereafter they usually produce one calf every two years, the calves suckling for many months, even where milk production is a priority.

The farmer will tether the yak and allow the calf to suckle for a while to stimulate milk let-down. The calf is then tethered nearby while the farmer milks the cow. Yields are not high in volume, but the milk is extraordinarily rich, with a butterfat content up to 16%, which contrasts favourably with 6.2% from a good Jersey cow. In some areas pasteurisation plants have been set up, although in remote areas this is plainly impossible. Butter and cheese keep well in the cold mountain air and are

Riding yaks

less bulky to transport than milk, so the farmers need make only a few journeys down each summer to bring their produce to the towns and villages.

Cheeses of types called Takchu and Choiga are made in summer time and stored for some time to dry, often within the security of a tent to prevent birds such as choughs getting at them. Cheese of the variety called Cheng is cut into squares with a hole in the middle, so that it can be carried on a piece of cord, the cheese being dried so that it is as hard as stone and virtually indestructible.

Yaks will carry loads of 100kg with ease, and the journeys down to the larger villages are jolly occasions, with the opportunity to drink chang and play dice with old friends – a welcome break for herders who may be on their own for months at a time on the higher summer pastures.

Farmers regularly vaccinate and worm their yaks. Mineral salt supplement is vital to the diet in areas where iodine deficiency is common, and during the latter part of pregnancy the cow yaks are fed extra rations in the form of wet mashes of rice, atta and some gure. During the winter months hay and rice straw are fed. The yak wool is gathered in July when shearing takes place. The wool is a valuable commodity used to make coats, socks and hats, tent coverings and ropes. I possess a yak hair halter, which is four-ply and very strong. These halters will last for more than twenty years, and are very 'kind' to the skin of the animal haltered. They also pull up incredibly quickly.

Disease control in yaks is difficult, given that the herds are scattered over remote mountain pastures for much of the year, with few facilities for catching or handling them. Gid is not uncommon. The disease is caused by the presence of the cyst stage of a dog tapeworm, which forms in the brain of the yak, causing it to stagger and walk in circles. Surgical removal is possible, but it is more practical to deworm the herd dogs regularly. Liverfluke disease, due to the trematode parasites *Fasciola hepatica* and *F.gigantica*, is common especially in the marshy areas where the snail vector occurs. Liver damage can be extensive: debilitated animals often die under the stress of winter conditions. Anthrax and rabies do occur, but at present the incidence is low. Animal husbandry is of a good standard in most areas, the yaks being well treated and much loved by their owners, not just because they are of value.

Reading Tshewang Rinzen's letter had rekindled my desire to revisit Sikkim. I knew that I faced an uphill struggle to obtain the necessary permits to visit the northern region, but until I became involved with Indian bureaucracy the full enormity of the situation did not become clear. I well remember an occasion in Gangtok when I was fulminating at some minor procedural idiocy, only to be brought up short by my friend Tashi Tobden: 'David. You must remember that your country taught my country bureaucracy!' Then, after a slight pause: 'But we have raised it to an art form!'

In the early summer I wrote to the Minister for Home Affairs in Delhi, and to the Secretary of State for Tourism in Sikkim, setting out my plans to go to Thanggu, over the Lungnak La into the Lhonak valley, and then over the Thay La south into the Zemu valley. From there I hoped to walk downriver to the confluence of the Zemu Chu with the Tista Chu at Lachen.

Five months passed with no response, so in February 1988 I sought the advice of Tim Renton MP (now Lord Renton), who at the time was minister with responsibility for Indian affairs. He very kindly wrote to the British High Commissioner in Delhi to see if there was anything he could do to help, but by May no progress had been made. Then in June I received an encouraging letter from the Indian consular office in London, and formally applied for a visa to visit Sikkim.

About that time my good friend Sir Edward Peck, himself a distinguished diplomat and alpinist, wrote to the British High Commissioner in Delhi, Sir David Goodall, to press my case. He also put me in touch with the very helpful librarian of the Alpine Club, who dug out all sorts of useful information on past climbing expeditions to

Sikkim. Encouraging sounds from various departments led me to contact Rajesh Lakhotia in Gangtok, to warn my three friends that I might after all get to Sikkim, and to lay ground plans for our trek.

In September the British High Commissioner in Delhi confirmed that permission for me to visit north Sikkim was forthcoming. The Indian Minister of Home Affairs had been on the point of refusing permission, and had it not been for the intervention of Sir David Goodall, Sir Edward Peck and Tim Renton that would have been the end of the matter. I shall always be deeply in debt to their kindness and persistence.

Although the expedition was still months away, I now started in earnest to garner every scrap of information I could get on north-west Sikkim. In particular I am grateful for the advice and information I received from Peter Carter, then second

Lachen village, the proposed destination of the author's second Sikkim journey

secretary at the British High Commission in Delhi, from Lord Hunt who had been in Lachen and to Khangchendzonga in 1937, and from Dr Geoffrey Neuss and Paul Orkney-Work, both of whom had climbed in that area.

David Long of the Royal Botanic Garden Edinburgh supplied me with a copy of the botanical survey by Smith and Cave in the Zemu and Lhonak valleys in 1911. My correspondence files were growing fatter daily, and I even managed to find a map of the area, albeit a fairly old one. It subsequently proved remarkably accurate and reinforced my admiration for the surveyors of the past. One big hurdle remained. Although my visa was issued in Britain, I should have to obtain the protected area permit in Delhi. Sound advice from Peter Carter warned me to allot several days for this.

The finer details of organisation within Sikkim had to wait until I reached Gangtok. Letters were taking weeks to reach their destination, indeed some never arrived, and telephones were unreliable. After two years of planning, however, it seemed that my dream of reaching the Lhonak valley might at last come true, and the early part of June passed in a flurry of activity, gathering all the bits and pieces of equipment vital for my purposes – photographic gear, sleeping bag, tent, protective clothing, reference books, plant collecting presses. I felt that I should need my own personal yak even to reach Heathrow.

I left for India on 21st June 1989, although under no illusions that I should reach my goal. It seemed more than likely that I might be turned back at Delhi, on entry into Sikkim, or at any stage north of Gangtok.

After all, I was travelling as an individual, I was not associated with any official organisation, and yet I was hoping to go into a restricted area where no one from the west had been for many years.

Indira Gandhi airport at midnight is not the most welcoming place, and I was glad to get to the Siddarth Hotel and seek refuge in sleep. Early next morning I telephoned the British High Commission, and was relieved to be told to expect H.B. Singh, the assistant Consular Officer, at 11am to sort out my permit applications.

Outside the heat was daunting. From my hotel window I could see hundreds of black kites, and high above them large numbers of white-backed vultures, soaring on the hot air currents rising above the city. Common mynahs and collared doves flocked in the hotel garden, and a single pure white cattle egret flapped past above the roaring traffic.

Cattle egret [Bruce Davidson/Nature Picture Library]

On the pavement opposite the hotel was a small tented encampment of Harayans. I watched one old lady spend hours carefully covering a large concrete street lamp base with sand, smoothing the surface and making a shallow circular pool in the centre. This she then carefully filled with water which she brought in polythene bags. Nothing whatsoever was ever done with her construction, which dried out and crumbled away over the next few days.

H.B. Singh arrived, a cheerful and most efficient Sikh, and quickly registered his disapproval of my papers, which he felt were barely adequate, although they had been issued by the Indian High Commission in London. He went off armed with every document and letter I possessed, promising to do his best.

At his suggestion I contacted the Botanical Survey of India, and late in the afternoon I took a taxi across Delhi to their offices in the Lodi Road. These proved to be a most depressing concrete block, very run down and with filthy corridors. Armed soldiers were everywhere, and I needed dozens of chits to get in to see the people I wanted. The director and his staff were very pleasant, but scarcely encouraging to my hopes of reaching north Sikkim. At that stage I had not realised how tight the military control was of north Sikkim, nor how few of their own scientists had ever been there or done any field work north of Gangtok.

Back at the hotel I found a message awaiting me from Rajesh, to say that all was well at their end. They had also asked K.C. Pradhan, the Chief Secretary of Sikkim, to write personally to the Ministry of Home Affairs in Delhi, to ensure that things went smoothly. There was also a welcome note from H.B. Singh, to say he had managed to arrange all the necessary permits.

Next morning was spent in a call to the British High Commission to collect my

Above left: Rose-ringed parakeet

Above right: Red-wattled lapwing

documents and briefly to see the consul, who warned me of the sort of problems I was likely to encounter in a restricted area. With time to kill, I went to the nearby Nehru Gardens, a real oasis of wildlife in the city centre. All around hoopoes were feeding their large fat youngsters, plunging their curved beaks deep into the lawns for worms and grubs. Where the gardeners had left a hose running a large puddle attracted collared doves, common, pied and Brahminy mynahs. Indian robins, the males all black with a white wing spot, the females dowdy brown, bounced around with tails cocked up in the air, while striped ground squirrels scampered up and down the trees.

More exciting to see were the wood-shrikes, coloured a delicate smoky grey with pale crown and dark mask, swooping like swallows from tree to tree, and exquisite purple sunbirds with iridescent plumage sipping nectar from the flowers. Red-wattled lapwings paraded solemnly in the open spaces, while overhead large green parakeets and house swifts were screaming and screeching. For any naturalists stuck in Delhi with time on your hands, remember the Nehru Gardens.

On my first evening I had wandered out to the hotel swimming pool where a children's swimming lesson was in progress, and met a most charming elderly Brahmin, M.V.S. Prakashrao, who was there to keep an eye on his young grandson. I had arranged to meet him again after lunch, when he presented me with a pot of his homemade fig jam, which was delicious, and an invitation to dine with him, his daughter and son-in-law that evening. This presented me with something of a problem: what would be the correct gift for a dinner

guest to take to the house of a Brahmin family? The hotel lobby manager came to my rescue, directing me to a local sweet shop which sold the most incredibly gooey and delicious looking concoctions I had ever seen. Armed with a large box of these sweets, I went to my friend's flat, where I was warmly welcomed by his family and spent a delightful evening. I have a weakness for mangoes, which must be one of the most delicious fruits in the world. My hosts shared this passion, and had lined up three different types for me to sample. Their favourite, and mine, was Langara, grown near Benares, with a green skin and splendid aromatic flavour. Next was Dashari, grown near Lucknow, yellow skinned and sweeter, but not so full of flavour. Finally there was Alfanso, grown near Mumbai. These were large, with red-tinged skin. They are a major export item, but were inferior to both the previous types. A fourth type, which we did not try, is called Chausa. This is very fibrous and is crushed to extract the juice. Street vendors will prepare this for you for a few rupees.

Later in the evening Rajesh telephoned from Gangtok to warn me that I might have problems taking photographs in north Sikkim, even of plants, and he advised me to get a letter of recommendation from the Botanical Survey of India in Delhi. Next morning I tried to get the recommended letter, but no one seemed willing or able to issue it without recourse to higher authority, which naturally could not be contacted. No problem!

Another desperately hot day, the slightest exertion causing soaked clothing, a misery compounded by an attack of the dreaded Delhi belly. Life in these circumstances tends to revolve around Lomotil and the nearest toilet, which rather cramps your style.

After a disturbed night, there followed the customary gruesome early start in the dark, and the drive by taxi to the internal flight to Bagdogra. I was unaware that there were now two domestic airports, and was left by my taxi-driver at the wrong one. At that unearthly hour no taxis were to be found and time was running out for my flight, so I grabbed a baggage trolley, filled it with all my gear, and was soon pounding up the road towards the other airport a good mile away.

An ambulance drew up beside me, and a cheerful doctor enquired if he could help? Learning of my predicament he jumped out, exclaiming 'These buggers are always doing this. Quick! Get in!' He then piled all my luggage into the ambulance, threw the baggage trolley into the ditch and drove me at high speed to the airport. No problem! As a means of getting through traffic an ambulance is to be strongly recommended.

The airport was utter chaos, with long queues stretching in all directions, morose security police and humidity near a hundred per cent. Take off was delayed for more than an hour, while we sat dripping in a stifling aeroplane with no air conditioning.

The flight to Bagdogra was through thick cloud and turbulence, a forewarning of the rapidly approaching monsoon. It cleared just before we reached our destination, but away to the south-west were massed ranks of purple and black storm clouds. The river Tista was in spate, and one section of the road between Rongphu and Singtam had slid down into the valley, leaving a raw gash in the hillside, across which we drove with the greatest care.

White-backed vulture

The next few days in Gangtok were endlessly frustrating, my mood swinging between elation when all appeared to be going well and despair when yet another problem reared its head. Wangyal and Rajesh had arranged for me to visit the Gangtok branch of the Botanical Survey of India, where I met the director and his assistant. I had taken a copy of a book I had written some years earlier on British orchids as evidence of my interests and capabilities. This was admired and everyone was most helpful, inviting me to revisit them when we returned from the Lhonak valley, but nothing in the way of a permit or letter of recommendation was forthcoming.

Back at the hotel we were greeted by bad news. The local army commander would not acknowledge the permits which I had brought from Delhi, although they clearly stated that I was permitted to study the flora in north Sikkim and set out the route by which I could travel. Wangyal and Rajesh accompanied me to the local army headquarters, where every possible argument was raised to obstruct our

Gangtok

journey. All departments denied having heard anything from Delhi. If we were to set out we should certainly be stopped and the use of a camera was likely to be forbidden. Wangyal and Rajesh then visited the Home Department, and after much persuasion obtained a permit for me from the Secretary of State, confirming that I was permitted to travel 'without let or hindrance' on the approved route.

To add to our sorrows we learned that Thanggu and the Lhonak valley had experienced very heavy snowfalls, which had blocked the roads and led to the death of many yaks and even some people. These reports were unconfirmed, so that we did not know if they had been designed to put us off.

We spent the evening at Wangyal's family home, a lovely old colonial style house on the ridge above Gangtok, set in a spacious garden. His father had been senior Sikkimese official in charge at Gyantse when Lowell Thomas made his journey to Lhasa. The family had kept a book of historic photographs taken at the time, which it was fascinating to see. They told me many stories about the area, some involving Sikkimese legends. One explains why rhododendrons are to be found close to ash trees. According to legend the rhododendron fell in love with the ash tree, but was forbidden to marry her. Overcome with grief he committed suicide by leaping over the rocks to where the ash tree grew below, and from that day rhododendrons are always to be found growing by ash trees. Another story involved the custom of young girls being ceremonially married to a pipal tree, *Ficus religiosa*. Later they may marry in normal fashion to a mere mortal.

I awoke at 3am to a bad attack of claustrophobia, brought on by the heat and humidity which made breathing a problem, for if I threw the windows open the mosquitos poured in and had a good meal at my expense. Soon after 4am the bazaar awoke, and at 6am I went out on the hotel roof, to be greeted by a wonderful view of Khangchendzonga in the light of early dawn. From Gangtok it looked like an immense tent of ice towering up into a pale blue sky, a sight to banish all ones problems. Little did I realise that this was to be the last time on the trip that I was to see a mountain top clearly.

I spent the morning around the Lal Bazaar, before we all met up to check out provisions and gear for our journey. I am usually fairly accommodating about what I eat, but I drew the line at the 'Chinese sausages' which Wangyal had provided: there is no point in inviting food poisoning before you start. I think he was a trifle disappointed at their rejection.

In the afternoon I walked out to the Dudul chorten at the Namgyal Institute of Tibetology at Deorali. The name features in many lists of plants collected at the turn of the century, and it is still a pleasant place of forest trees and flowers. The Nam-nang road drops steeply down through terraced hillsides, and on the roadside I found plenty of plants to interest me,

In the Lal Bazaar

Gonatanthus pumilus

including the cobra-lily *Arisaema tortuosum*, nearly 1m tall, with purple spotted stem, broad fingered leaves and a hooded flower with a long appendage raised up like an elephant's trunk. Around the chorten the trees bore many fascinating epiphytic plants, among which were the orchid *Coelogyne flaccida*, with tiny white flowers, *Hoya lanceolata* with drooping umbels of pink flowers like sugar icing, scarlet *Agapetes serpens* and *Gonatanthus pumilus* with heart-shaped leaves patterned with purple. Growing on the side of the path was a curious plant, *Houttuynia cordata*, the flower consisting of four white petal-like bracts, at the centre of which was a large gold coloured boss of anthers and trifid stigmas. The local people eat it with chillies and cheese.

We set off at last on 28th June after an early breakfast. Heavy overnight rain had stopped: Khangchendzonga was briefly visible before everything was obliterated by low cloud. Our two jeeps were packed to the roof with the four of us, our cook Ashun and a mountain of gear. Our route lay north out of Gangtok along the North Sikkim Highway, which curves and plunges over the deeply folded hillsides. Beside the road we passed a pair of prayer wheels housed in huts like miniature gompas. A stream was diverted to turn a paddlewheel sited under each prayer wheel, so that

Namgyal gompa, Dudul chorten

Aeschynanthus sikkimensis

the prayers contained in it could be offered up continuously. We heard a whistling thrush singing loudly nearby, while his mate was busy feeding their young in a nest in the bank of the stream.

We drove on for hours to our first halt at a teahouse on the banks of the Bakcha Chu run by the family of Tsering Bhutia. The family were old friends of my companions, who used to come fishing in the river. The teahouse was absolutely spotless, the shelves lined with gleaming copper pans, presided over by Grandma, a diminutive but dynamic little Sikkimese lady. My friends told me that if they were late up for their tea, a small child was dispatched to summon them, and woe betide if they failed to come! Grandma eyed me up and down with a twinkle in her eye – I was the first westerner who had ever been in her teahouse. I was then introduced to her son, his pretty wife and their two children, a little girl and a very small baby boy with wide brown eyes.

The next stretch of our journey took us through a series of small villages, the whole area near the road being terraced and intensively cultivated with crops of rice, maize, potatoes and squashes. It is always a problem to identify plants and birds from a wildly bucking jeep, but I managed to catch fleeting glimpses of black-capped sibias, Tibetan shrikes, robin dayal and two young steppe eagles. I did persuade the driver to stop for the eagles, which were soaring at tree-top level just above the road, and at the same time found the orchid *Otochilus fuscus* growing on a moss covered rock. The flowers, about a dozen in number, were carried in an elegant spray, all the petals and sepals slender and pure white, with a dagger-shaped lip bearing deep orange blotches at the base.

The road now twisted and turned, climbing up the steep hillsides before plunging down to the river Tista at the bottom of the valley, which grew ever deeper and deeper. When we reached Mangan we called at the new offices of the government of North District Sikkim, where Wangyal spent some time obtaining further permits from the chief of police. At the same time we learned that Thanggu, and thus the Lhonak valley, had been totally cut off by very deep and unseasonable snow, and that hundreds of yaks had died of cold and starvation, stranded by the bad weather on their summer grazings. The police suggested we press on as far as Lachen, and obtain more up to date information there.

During our halt at Mangan I spent some time with C.P. Tongden, assistant engineer in the Rural Development Department, and a friend of Lekshed. He had a particular interest in the medicinal use of native plants, and I wished that I could have spent more time with him. I learned that the root of *Bergenia ciliata* (Pakhan Bait) is dried, crushed and ground into a paste to treat footrot in cattle. The juice of one species of *Artemesia* is poured into rivers to stupefy fish, and the crushed leaves can be stuffed up the nose as a cure for epistaxis –

Water-powered prayer wheel

Tshering Bhutia family at Bakcha Chu

Otochilus fuscus, found growing on a moss-covered rock

Near Mangan

nosebleed! As a sufferer, I can vouch for the fact that it works quickly and well.

The road now started to climb higher, frequently crossed by cascades of water which threatened to sweep our jeeps over the edge. At times the road ran below overhanging cliffs, so that we drove underneath the waterfalls. Keeping the road system open is a fearful task, and the route was lined by the shacks of the road repair gangs, mainly Biharis. Their living conditions looked primitive, but even then are better than they could expect at home. Small groups of women sat under barely adequate awnings made of plastic sheets, breaking rocks into fragments suitable for road building. Others worked in pairs, one with a shovel, the other pulling a short rope attached to it to give it more purchase.

Once again I attempted to identify birds and plants as we bounced merrily along, this time managing to see elegant hair-crested drongos perched on the telephone wires, and large racquet-tailed drongos with incredibly long wire-like outer tail feathers with tips like little black flags. We also saw a hoary bar-wing, a jay-sized bird, brown striped with a punk hairstyle. In mid-afternoon we reached Tsunthang, where we crossed a large bridge into the town at the confluence of the Tista and Lachung rivers, each running in a welter of foam in a deep gorge.

From now on our route followed the winding course of the Tista, here running in a flat valley bottom bounded to the east by steep cliffs. There were quite extensive stretches of oak forest, and tall trees of *Castanopsis hystrix* covered in creamy coloured flower spikes, under which were growing bushes of *Brassaiopsis mitis* with huge ten-fingered leaves and masses of round flower heads like gigantic ivy flowers. It was now drizzling heavily, so we could see little of the view. We stopped for a short break several miles south of Lachen on a steep hillside, with the turbulent river far below in the gathering dusk. The broken slopes were carpeted with tall yellow *Euphorbia sikkimense*, bushes of *Hydrangea altissima* with unopened buds of dark navy blue, and the fragrant white *Deutzia compacta*. Far up above us I could just see clumps of the impressive 2m-tall lily *Cardiocrinum giganteum*, with drooping white flowers. These have a sweet scent which can be appreciated a long way off. By now the light was too poor for photography and we reached Lachen in darkness and dripping mist.

There was a large, well built dak bungalow, where we installed ourselves once we had rooted out the chowkidar from his home some distance away, and we

retired to bed by candlelight. Once more I was smitten by an attack of claustrophobia, made worse when a cat leaped through the window I had flung open, and on to my sleeping bag. It then proceeded to tear around the room like a wall-of-death rider, before disappearing by the same route as that by which it had come. Claustrophobia is a devastating affliction, and it does not help one whit to know in the reasoning part of your mind that it is unreasonable behaviour. The feeling of panic and the need to get out are totally overwhelming. At dawn I could no longer control it, and woke up Rajesh to explain that I felt dreadful and wanted to return home. The poor chap must have wondered what sort of nutcase he was landed with, and it is to his eternal credit that he talked me through it, and the mere fact that someone else knew what I felt helped greatly.

Lachen is rather a forlorn place. It consists of several hundred houses set on a flat area bounded on all sides by steep cliffs, the mainly wooden houses built up on short stilts above a muddy street with a stream running through it. Messages had been sent ahead to try to ascertain the weather and road conditions up to Thanggu. They were fairly reasonable in Lachen, if somewhat damp and dreary, and it appeared that traffic was able to go north. Eventually we were allowed to walk out of the village to the west, past a rather nice school and a small but pretty gompa. However, we had an armed escort and no photographs were allowed. This was enormously frustrating, as the steep terraced hillside was a mass of wild flowers and full of interesting birds. The walk uphill was steep and hot, with leeches everywhere on the rocks and bushes.

Waterfall near Mangan

Lachen village

Calanthe alpina

Mertensia moltkioides, yellow *Viola biflora*, purple *Roscoea auriculata* and a delightful orchid, *Calanthe alpina*. This had scented yellow green flowers with a purple striped lip, but I had to kneel down to appreciate its beauty. The leeches were soon all over my boots and clothes.

Our armed escort got bored and disappeared, so we pushed on higher up the hill, where I found an old gnarled tree literally dripping with orchids, in this case the white flowered *Pleione hookeriana* and a second species which closely resembled *P.humilis*. Oh, for a camera!

The bird life of Lachen was equally diverse, with rufous turtledoves, black drongos, crossbills, Nepal sunbirds, greenish and Pallas's warblers, a flock of red-tailed minlas and a tree alive with both scarlet and long-tailed minivets. All the time we were shadowed by a pair of black eagles. The rain then came down in torrents, so we retreated to the bungalow and drowned our sorrows in tots of Sikkimese brandy and hot water.

The next morning was not auspicious. Thick low cloud and drizzle obscured everything, the nozzle on the kerosene cooker was blocked, and there was a total ban on photography. While I waited, the bell rang for the school on the hillside opposite, the buildings and attendant prayer flags silhouetted against the low clouds. I could see little figures toiling up the slope and one group of children singing in the rain, with another tiny figure vigorously conducting them. Most of the village houses are built up on stilts, with wide verandahs and galvanised tin roofs. Firewood and fodder for the animals are stacked beneath the houses, and around

To stop, even for a second, was to invite an invasion of the little pests, while we were attacked by hoards of tiny flies with a vicious bite. Despite this, the flowers at Lachen were truly wonderful.

The hills up behind the Lachen gompa are very steep, rocky and heavily grazed, with deep wooded gullies running down the upper slopes. It was in these more inaccessible places that the best flowers were to be found. Just behind the gompa was a massive bush of *Rosa macrophylla* fully 8m high, covered with pinkish purple flowers. Nearby I found pink *Rosa micrantha*, white *R.moschata*, bushes of *Spiraea arcuata*, yellow flowered *Berberis angulosa*, sweet scented *Viburnum grandiflorum* and *Philadelphus tomentosus*, and leathery leaved *Gaultheria fragrantissima*. Underneath the trees we found the cobra lilies *Arisaema intermedia*, *A.jacquemontii* and *A.griffithii*, the Solomon's seals *Polygonatum cirrhifolium* and purple flowered *P.cathcartii*, blue

them are stone walled vegetable plots. Water runs everywhere, even the big village prayer wheel being water powered. Lachen is very scruffy, and Lekshed, with his professional interest, would have loved to replan it.

We finally set off at 10am with water everywhere, running down the road and cascading over the cliffs. There were some fine stands of *Abies densa*, with the tall white lily *Cardiocrinum giganteum* gleaming under them in the gloom. Near Thombu we paused briefly beside some lovely water meadows set below pine covered cliffs, looking like a Chinese landscape painting. This would make a good camping site and appeared botanically interesting. Near Yakthang there were some fine meadows carpeted with tall yellow *Primula sikkimensis*, pale flowered *P.dickeana* and the little purple orchid *Chusua pauciflora*, but the presence of a military camp nearby meant that we could not stop to look at the flowers, and certainly could not take photographs.

The sun came out at last, sending flocks of alpine choughs spiralling up into the sky, and we saw our first yaks grazing on a hillside covered with mauve *Primula capitata*. In the early afternoon we finally reached Thanggu. The village could not have changed much since Hooker was there in 1849. It consisted of about a dozen little shingle roofed farmhouses set in a patch-work of tiny, stone walled vegetable fields, over which towered a huge glacial erratic boulder. This is well portrayed in the engravings which are in Hooker's Himalayan Journals, where he notes 'A stupendous rock, about fifty feet high, lay in the middle of the valley, broken in two.' It is still called Hooker's Rock.

Above: Pleione hookeriana

Right: Chusua pauciflora

Below right: Pleione aff.humilis

Nearby, however, was a large army camp, and the place teemed with soldiers. There is now a comfortable dak bungalow, but it was some time before we were sure that we should be allowed to stay there. It was made obvious that my presence was most unwelcome, and that the unit commander would be much happier if I went away. However, having been to so much trouble to obtain all the necessary permission from the governments of both India and the state of Sikkim, I was in no mood to accede to his demands and return to Gangtok. He in turn was equally determined to make it as awkward for me as possible, so I was forbidden to leave the bungalow, even to walk around the village, and my camera and binoculars were taken away. The other problem was that the plumbing in the bungalow was non-functional, which necessitated a walk under escort up the

road to the nearest rocks to find any seclusion. A fairly severe bout of enteritis usually resulted in a somewhat undignified gallop up the road, with the military escort trailing behind. The fact that his rifle was fully loaded, and the safety catch was off, did not add to my sense of well-being. It only needed an itchy trigger finger, some inadvertent noises from me, and one had the ingredients for a small disaster!

The bungalow at Thanggu is well sited above the north end of the village, with splendid views out across the valley to the upper Tista river. Just above is a small gompa with several Tibetan-style chortens, while behind the hill sweeps up another 1000m with a line of prayer flags stretching across it. The lower slopes are clothed with birch trees and rhododendron up to the sky line, although to the west across the river there is evidence of extensive tree felling and subsequent erosion. Outside on the verandah an old woman was spinning wool, while another worked at a small hand

Meadow at Tsoptha

loom. Overhead small skylarks sang, and a large pied wagtail strutted on the grass. It was so frustrating to see the flower-covered hillsides and the gompa just above me, all inviting exploration, and yet to be stuck inside the bungalow.

Meanwhile Wangyal and the others were busy arguing with the army personnel to get clearance to cross the Lungnak La into the Lhonak valley. It wasn't just bloody-mindedness on the part of the military, for severe snow conditions were reported on the highest 3km section of the pass. Sheep as well as yaks had died in the recent storms, driven by starvation to eat each other's wool. Unconfirmed reports said that people had also been killed. Slowly opposition eased, leaving Wangyal trying to organise porters or yaks to help us carry our gear to Muguthang in two days' time. A police party was due to cross, and it was suggested that we should go with them for safety. Apparently once over the pass the route was clear of snow all the way west to Goma. I was very well aware that without the tireless efforts of my friends, our trip to the Lhonak valley would have ended in total failure and a return to Gangtok.

In the late afternoon we were allowed to walk out across the Tista by a tree-trunk bridge just north of Hooker's Rock to the hillside opposite. This was terraced like a rock garden, carpeted with primulas and dwarf rhododendrons, with little streams of crystal clear water trickling down and bright green bogs dotted with flowers. In our brief walk I found *Primula sikkimensis*, *P.capitata* and *P.denticulata*, pink *Rhododendron setosum* and the yellow and pink forms of *R.anthopogon*, the butterwort *Pinguicula alpina*, the bright yellow lousewort

Pedicularis longiflora

Pedicularis longiflora with extraordinary tubular shaped flowers, and three terrestrial orchids *Malaxis muscifera*, the little mauve *Chusua pauciflora* and the butterfly orchid *Platanthera arcuata*. We identified at least thirty other flowering plants, and I began to wonder if it would be possible to get any photographs of this floral wonderland. The cold and wet closed in again and we retreated indoors, where Rajesh had got a good log fire going.

Next morning there were just a few postage stamp-sized bits of blue sky, although it still drizzled. The chief of police turned up, and was charming and helpful: 'Mr Lang, why do you not go and photograph your flowers while it is fine? Be sensible, and do not point your camera near the army camp.'

I needed no further bidding, and was across the log bridge and up the slope like a jack rabbit. I was soon spotted by the army, and could see them fanned out across the slope below me, blowing whistles and

Cypripedium himalaicum

Saussurea obvallata

shouting. I had made a mental note from the day before of the plants I wished to photograph, and ran from plant to plant getting every picture I could before they caught up with me. Oddly enough they did not expose the film, although they took my camera again. As I was marched back past the police chief, he smiled wanly – a kindly man overruled by the wretched local commander.

Although I was now camera-less, we did manage to set out for the day, crossed the river and walked up through the forest to a valley running north-west from Thanggu. The initial climb was steep and rough, through pine trees and dense rhododendron scrub. Tiny annual gentians were scattered everywhere, like little blue jewels in the grass, and at about 4500m we found the blue poppy *Meconopsis simplicifolia* in abundance. As we emerged above the tree line onto a more barren slope we found a bank covered in beautiful slipper orchids. *Cypripedium himalaicum* bears really big flowers, often two to a stem, candy-striped in red and maroon. The sight of several hundred massed together was stunning. In the same area were sheets of *Primula capitata*, purple flowers contrasting with pale green leaves and stems dusted with white farina, and tight clumps of tiny *Primula muscoidea*.

We walked on up to a peak at about 5200m through a veritable sea of mauve, white and pink dwarf rhododendrons, purple and green orchids, and thousands of mauve and green flowered lilies and fritillaries. At the summit my friends performed a puja for the success of our trek, making a small fire on which we burned fragrant twigs of juniper and rhododendron. We needed every scrap of good fortune we could get, so all our prayers were heartfelt.

Crossing the mountain ridge we walked up the north side of a long river valley running north-west, until we came to a series of small waterfalls. Here grew the giant rhubarb *Rheum nobile* with flowers stems 2m tall draped in huge cream coloured bracts, as well as a profusion of sky blue flowers – *Corydalis ecristata*, *Gentiana humilis* and the tiny *G.bryoides*. *Saussurea obvallata* was plentiful. This is a strange plant with thistle-like flowers completely enveloped in big translucent bracts, as if the flower head had been tied up in a plastic bag. The bracts protect the flowers from the weather, but still allow insects to creep inside to pollinate the flowers. The root of the plant is used medicinally for stomach upsets. The walk

Arisaema jacquemontii

back was a real slog through knee-high, sopping wet rhododendrons, crossing and recrossing the river, until we finally descended to Thanggu soaked to the skin.

Back at camp we were offered some woollen Indian army issue balaclavas for sale at a very reasonable price, so I duly bought one. Alas, they were made for Indian heads, and mine is very large. The balaclava sat on top like a pea on a drum, to the great delight of my friends!

We arose early, with the chance to cross over the Lungnak La. We reduced all our gear to the minimum, and I left the telephoto lens and half my supply of film behind. Some photography of plants was permitted, but no views of the countryside. This was an improvement on a total ban. The weather was not marvellous, and an overnight fall of snow had dusted even the lower hilltops, but we felt it was worth a try. About 2km north of Thanggu the track crossed the Tista by a bridge, then turning due west following a lovely valley with steep cliffs on the south side and a river meandering along the valley floor. Here the track was good, climbing gently up the north flank of the valley. Beside the path flowered *Fritillaria cirrhosa*, orange snake's-head flowers spotted with green, green cobra lilies *Arisaema jacquemontii*, blue *Meconopsis simplicifolia* and a carpet of dark-eyed, purple flowered *Primula macrophylla*.

The path became steeper and rougher, skirting two mist shrouded lakes, and then entered a series of very steep zigzags. *Rheum nobile* grew plentifully there, and our porters cut off a spike, peeled it and gave me the central stem to chew. It is a great thirst quencher, astringent and pleasant tasting. We reached the summit of the

Lungnak La after five hours, both Lekshed and I feeling shattered. At 6000m we found it quite difficult to concentrate on what we wanted to do, and I found it hard to focus my eyes on any object close to me. Visibility in the thick cloud and drizzle was virtually nil, so we did not linger. The descent on the west side is impressive, a 60° slope deep in snow and very slippery. We all fell over many times on our way down, having no crampons or ice axes. After a descent of 700m we came down into a cwm ringed by black cliffs, where there was lake, the Chabro Tso. This was about 600m long, clear and cold, the water totally devoid of any plant life. Among the rocks nearby I did find a few clumps of *Primula primulina* – mauve flowers with a throat packed with white hairs – while around us a flock of Brandt's mountain finches were busy feeding, running about among the rocks like little white mice.

The Lungnak La is not an easy pass even in good weather, and for much of the year it

Riding yak at Muguthang

Top: *Arenaria bryophylla*

Above: *Polygonatum hookeri*

pieces studded with cowrie shells, brass bells and tufts of red and blue wool. It was soon explained to me that Wangyal and Lekshed were the first government officials to visit Muguthang for twenty seven years, and that I was probably the first botanist there since the days of Smith and Cave in 1909. While cheerful greetings were being exchanged, a large avalanche thundered down the cliffs to the south.

We then rode down in state to the village. This was my first ride on a yak and was great fun – rather like riding on a big furry armchair – although on the steep bits it was a trifle disconcerting to look down past the horns to the ground, which seemed rather a long way off. Steering was effected by a single rope through the yak's nostrils, which combined with the very short stirrups made me feel a trifle insecure. As we descended the steep path, we moved through acres of red, white and purple rhododendrons. On the barer slopes grew green cushions of *Arenaria bryophylla* and *A.ciliolata*, masses of the eidelweiss *Leontopodium fimbrilligerum*, and several species of anemone which I was unable to examine, as my yak would not stop!

At the village we were met by the elders and draped in white silk scarves in greeting. We were then seated on carpets and served Tibetan tea, which I found very much to my liking. Forget the old calumny of rancid yak butter: this tea was piping hot, made with salt and fresh butter, and served in handle-less cups fitted with lids. When you consider, butter tea is a most sensible beverage to drink at high altitude. Tea acts as a mild stimulant, butter gives you energy and salt replaces the electrolytes lost in sweating. Although at home I rarely drink more than

is not possible to use yaks to cross it. Certainly it would be a bad place to get caught in a storm, although police and army personnel do the trip in most months of the year. It was an odd feeling to realise that the last westerners to stand in this place were British climbers on their way back from the Zemu glacier in 1936.

To my great surprise we found a deputation of villagers gathered by the lake with four riding yaks, gaily caparisoned and ready for us to use. To this day I do not know how they knew that we were coming, but they had obviously come all the way up to this desolate spot to welcome us. The yaks were a wonderful sight, saddles covered in richly coloured carpets, collars and head one cup of tea at a sitting, I found myself downing half a dozen butter teas with alacrity.

The people of the Lhonak valley were all Tibetan, with little affinity with the residents of Thanggu and Lachen. Although nominally in Sikkim, as a result of state boundaries drawn in the days of the raj, they have in reality been left to care for themselves. We now heard what had happened in the recent storms, and why they were so keen for word of their distress to get back to government through the good offices of my friends. In recent weeks they had lost more than 200 yaks and 600 sheep from snow and starvation, a very grave loss for a small isolated community. The heavy snowfall had also led to the collapse of some house roofs in the village, although no one had died.

The village schoolmaster spoke very good English, so I was interested to learn of the problems they encountered with their yaks. Just as at Lingshi in Bhutan, the main diseases that troubled them were liver fluke and hydatid cysts. This was not surprising, as there were extensive marshes just below the village where many yaks were grazing.

We rode on from the village for another 3km to a border police post, where we were billeted. This was simple in construction, built around a square, with a verandah and a superb view westwards up the Lhonak valley towards Khangchendzonga. On the south side of the wide valley we could just see the snow-bound pass of the Thay La, which the locals assured us was quite impassable. They had set up two tall stone cairns on the pass, and could see from several miles away how deep the snow was at the crossing point. This meant that our plans to travel over the Thay La to the Zemu valley were clearly impossible, and we should have to restrict our studies to the Lhonak valley only.

We were up next morning early and had a good wash in the spring which gushes out of the mountainside right beside the police post. I was still affected by the altitude, and had some difficulty in focussing my eyes. The weather was reasonable and some of the glaciers and snow slopes were just beginning to appear through the cloud. Wangyal was up before any of the rest of us, and was busy doing fifty press-ups before breakfast. It made me breathless just to look at him.

Like all areas on the edge of the Tibetan plateau, Muguthang is not rich in bird numbers, but the birds that do live there are interesting and incredibly tame. Tibetan twite, common rosefinch and Brandt's mountain finch were all hopping around the verandah at our feet. Alas, my camera

Dolmasampa

was still in purdah. The short turf around our camp was a colourful carpet of dwarf flowers, purple *Lancea tibetica*, blue *Oxytropis lapponica, Arenaria ciliolata, Draba tibetica*, pink *Polygonatum hookeri* and yellow *Ranunculus adoxifolius*.

I did get leave to go for a short walk down the valley to a marshy area at the foot of the slope on which we camped. Here tussocks of grass were studded with *Primula tibetica* like pink jewels, and to my surprise I found masses of *Glaux maritima*, which in Britain we know as Sea Milkwort – the last thing I expected to find at 5000m on the Tibetan plateau. This was the best area locally for birds, which included horned

Another view of Dolmasampa

lark, snow finch, Altai and red-breasted accentors, alpine chough, nesting redshank, a ruddy shelduck with nine ducklings and, best of all, the strange little bird called Hume's groundpecker. These were pale brown in colour with a fairly long curved beak, and bounced about among the yak turds which they flicked over with nonchalant expertise to grab the worms and insects under them. It would have been easy to photograph them, as they were tame and approachable, but my camera was still unavailable.

We were given a conducted tour of the village, where many houses had been severely damaged by the heavy snowfall. I soon located our yak men with some local farmers, as I was keen to know how much veterinary treatment was available to them. They were quite competent to give both intramuscular and subcutaneous injections, but had no idea of sterilising their equipment first. They did possess foot-and-mouth vaccine and some bottles of oxytetracycline, but they were years out of date. Their sheep had infectious keratoconjunctivitis, and several newly lambed ewes had gangrenous mastitis, so with the help of the schoolmaster I tried to put across some ideas of sterilising syringes, improving ventilation in the animal buildings and basic animal hygiene. I think it would take a lot of nagging and follow-up service to effect much change in their routine. Lunch was produced. Everything was spotlessly clean but so strongly laced with chillies that I simply could not eat it. Back at the police post I found some dates, dried apricots and chocolate, which had to suffice.

After some persuading I was allowed to walk down the valley in the direction of Dolmasampa, provided that I had an armed escort. Lekshed came with me. The valley floor near Muguthang is very flat, with a sandy, gritty soil dotted with small stones. Rounded hills spring abruptly from the edges of the plain, rising steeply into black cliffs, and finally massive snow peaks – when you can see them. Siniolchu to the south was absolutely beautiful, a white spire of the sort a child would draw to illustrate a snow mountain. We never saw it because of low cloud, but Wangyal returned to Muguthang the next year and sent me a picture of the peak.

The gravel plain looked sterile, but it was carpeted with sedges and tiny flowers. Three species which were most abundant were the minute lily-like *Lloydia serotina* with drooping creamy coloured flowers, the dwarf pink coloured *Polygonatum hookeri* and the little blue *Gentiana humilis*. Everything grows close to the ground or in a tight cushion to avoid being smashed or dessicated in the fierce winds.

Ang Dawa, the senior police officer, confirmed my ideas of the climate of the Lhonak valley. In winter it is often dry, but bitterly cold with immensely strong winds. He had seen stones weighing 2kg being bowled along by the wind. Lekshed and I turned up a small side valley to the north, where I could see rocky outcrops

Hume's ground-pecker

Lloydia serotina

Primula tibetica

which were not likely to be grazed. Here we found *Anemone polyanthes, Berberis wallichiana, Eritrichium acaule, Ribes luridum, Stellaria subumbellatum, Rheum spiciforme* and a mauve flowered, yellow-eyed primula, *Primula caveana*, named after one of my illustrious predecessors in this very valley.

Supper was inedible. It was not just my own dislike of very hot dishes, but the fact that our cook was hopeless. Even the dahl he produced could have doubled as jet fuel. The night was bad. I suffered from Cheynes-Stokes respiration and sleep apnoea. At high altitude the body responds

to the decreased oxygen content of the air by increasing the depth and rate of breathing. This leads to a drop in the level of carbon dioxide in the blood and alters the pH – a measure of acidity – of the blood. The body tries to compensate, raising the breathing rate sufficiently to increase blood oxygen and excreting bicarbonates to preserve the dwindling carbon dioxide. An area of the mid-brain responds to changes in pH and carbon dioxide, while the carotid bodies in the neck respond to changes in oxygen level. This dual control results in the erratic breathing pattern called Cheynes-Stokes

Yak men at Muguthang

respiration, where periods of rapid, increasingly deep breathing are followed by periods when breathing stops – often for an alarmingly long time. I awoke fighting for breath and had to force myself to inhale. Out of interest I checked my pulse rate, as my heart was revving like a motorbike, and found that it was 220 to the minute. As my breathing rhythm settled, so my pulse rate fell back towards normal, but as soon as I fell asleep the whole cycle was repeated. Lekshed suffered as well, although he normally lives at 3000m, much higher than my own home a mere 30m above sea level. We were both shattered by the time morning broke.

After breakfast I was invited to take photographs of the personnel and yaks, which naturally included the valley in the background. Life had an Alice-in-Wonderland quality! At 8am the riding yaks arrived, and we set off up the valley westwards. My yak promptly threw me, and I was dragged along with one boot still jammed in the stirrup. Apart from a broken watch and a few cuts and bruises, I was intact. I was allowed to take photographs of flowers, and found *Lloydia flavonutans* to add to the species recorded the previous day. We decided to walk, as the going was flat and the weather pleasant apart from a strong wind. We kept along the valley floor for some miles, crossing a side river at Dolmasampa by a substantial bridge. The track then climbed steeply up a huge moraine slope which lay right across the valley. Once over the top, the view was fantastic – a deep glacial valley with a raging river running along the bottom. The slopes above the river were composed of finely pulverised gneiss, like white dust, above

Approaching Rasung

which the rock faces swept up to vanish into clouds and snow. Everything was very dry, with cushion plants such as *Arenaria densissima*, *Androsace delavayi* and *Parrya platycarpa* wedged in among the rocks, where they had a modicum of protection.

We now rode along the edge of a steep slope, with a nearly vertical drop of 100m to the river below. There was no proper track, and the yak had to pick its way along the crumbly slope. To tell the truth, my eyes were tight shut.

At Rasung we stopped for a lunch break. This was a lovely site, open grassland dissected by clear streams, the turf studded with tiny primulas and gentians. Around us we could see vast black cliffs and tumbling glaciers, above which the icy spires of Tent Peak and Fluted Peak peered through the clouds. *Rhododendron setosum* and *R.nivale* grew on the rocks, and we could see a few spikes of the giant rhubarb on the slopes high above us. Here also we found evidence of the disaster which had befallen the local yaks. Fourteen carcases lay strewn around, and beside them the dessicated body of a young Himalayan griffon vulture – the only bird we saw in the upper Lhonak valley.

We rode on towards Goma, finding another forty dead yaks. On a pile of yak dung I found a large geostar fungus nearly 25cm in diameter. Here the river hugs the north side of the valley, running tumultuously between high gravel banks. Wangyal felt that it was his duty to cross to the other bank of the river, to check on a rumour of many more dead yaks. He and the senior yak man stripped their yaks and themselves of all unnecessary gear and plunged into the river. They barely made it across, with water up to the level of the saddles, and a current which nearly swept the yaks off their feet. We watched the tiny figures, dwarfed by the huge slope above them, as they struggled out of the river on the far side. My respect for *Bos grunniens* increased, to say nothing of the toughness of

Above right:
Saxifraga aristulata

Below: Upper Lhonak valley

their riders. We waited anxiously for their return, as the weather became threatening, with black skies to the west below Khangchendzonga and flurries of snow. I spent much of the time searching the gravel banks of the river for plants of interest, but the area was barren, obviously swept by flood water in winter. I did find *Saussurea uniflora*, the rue *Thalictrum squamifera* with tiny purple flowers, and the equally tiny *Artemesia desertorum*, *Myricaria rosea*, the buttercup *Ranunculus pulchellus*, small and covered in grey hairs, and *Saxifraga aristulata*. It was all very parched and windswept

Eventually the riders returned, soaked and cold, having indeed confirmed the local rumour of many dead yaks. There had been no exaggeration. We rode most of the way back to Muguthang, despite the fact that both Rajesh and I were thrown in the river by our recalcitrant mounts, and finished off with a wild race at Wangyal's instigation, our yaks galloping madly across the flat plain. It was a case of 'last one home pays for the beer', and I'm afraid to say that I was resoundingly last.

We sat around the fire until late in the evening, discussing what our next move should be. There was no way we could get out of the Lhonak valley south to the Zemu valley, and we were strictly limited in what we could do and where we could go. We should have to go back the way we had come, and over that difficult route it had been snowing every day since we had crossed the pass. It was also likely that we should be on our own, with no porters available to help us. Lekshed had a better night, but I was still troubled with breathing, and to add to my discomfort my hands and feet had swollen so badly that my fingers resembled sausages.

The police personnel at Muguthang were unfailingly kind and courteous throughout our stay, clearing out two of their own rooms to make space for us, and lighting fires to keep us warm. One of them, Ugyen, had been posted for four years at Muguthang, and he was full of fascinating information about the wildlife. Blue sheep - bharal - were not uncommon, but he also described the eastern subspecies of Marco Polo sheep, *Ovis ammon* ssp.*hodgsonii*. These had not been recorded since the days of Joseph Hooker, and I must admit that at the time I had some doubts of what he had seen. However, Sikkimese naturalists have since filmed a small flock in the area, and there is no doubt that they still breed in north Sikkim. Wolves were to be seen in most winters, but more intriguing were his reports of wild dogs which appeared in packs at the end of October, and were known to pull down and kill young yaks. He was adamant that they were neither jackals nor pi dogs, and that they had very large ears. I have since learned that they also occur in the Lunana area of northern Bhutan, where they are called Chungku,

which translates as 'single hunter'. They usually hunt alone, but can work as a pack. They tend to overkill more prey than they need. We simply do not know enough about

Top: Wangyal returns

Bottom: Watching the crossing of the river

Ugyen with bharal horns

Below right: Pedicularis oederi

Below: Rhododendron setosum

streams flowed into the main river. Among the rocks I found *Rhododendron setosum*, *R.lepidotum*, *R.camelliflorum*, *Berberis macrosepala*, *Ribes luridum*, *Pedicularis oederi*, *Leontopodium fimbrilligerum*, *Aster stracheyi* and *Morina betonicioides*. A big buttercup with red stems and red flushed flowers turned out to be *Trollius sikkimensis*.

The river looked beautiful, meandering across the floor of the valley, the banks bordered by broad swathes of mauve *Rhododendron setosum*. A single white-bellied dipper flew by. The view westward towards Khangchendzonga was breathtaking, even though the big peaks were still shrouded in cloud. We decided to get back by walking across the marsh, which involved hopping from tussock to tussock across a maze of water channels, but it was still worthwhile. The marsh plants included the kingcup *Caltha scaposa*, the butterwort *Pinguicula alpina*, *Lagotis clarkei*, *Astragalus yunnanensis* with yellow flowers partly enclosed in a chocolate brown calyx, *Saussurea uniflora*, *Onosma hookeri*, blue *Erytrichium pygmaeum* and the attractive little purple orchid *Aorchis spathulata*.

this remote area to be sure that we have recorded all the animals and birds it contains. For example, in 1996 breeding by black-necked cranes was confirmed in the Muguthang area. These birds are extremely rare, and this is a new extension of their known breeding range. They were certainly not there in 1989 when we were there, and one can only pray that they will be protected and encouraged in the future.

I was allowed out for a long walk with Ugyen as my escort, but no photography was permitted. We walked down from the camp to the valley floor and skirted the cliffs to the south towards the Lhonak Chu where it flows eastward out of the valley. Ugyen was enthusiastic and knowledgeable about the plant life. We managed to find the most productive areas where it was either too rocky for the herds to graze easily, or where the tributary

I got back to find that my friends had disappeared, and no one seemed to know where they had gone. My limited Gurkhali served no useful purpose, and I had to spend seven frustrating hours cooped up in the police post until they returned. They had managed to walk up to the Khora La on the ridge east of the main Lhonak valley, where they collected specimens of the spiny blue poppy *Meconopsis horridula*, the extraordinary woolly *Saussurea gossypiphora*, *Primula macrophylla*, *Corydalis ecristata* and *Saxifraga pilifera*. I rather wished that I had been able to go with them.

I spent another thoroughly miserable night, my problems made worse by a severe attack of dysentery, which left me feeling weary. We left camp at 7am in cold and mist, the weather threatening to dump yet more snow on us. No porters or yaks were available, as all the villagers were celebrating the Dalai Lama's birthday, but Ugyen and the senior officer of the Muguthang police post, the charming and kindly Ang Dawa, came with us. They were travelling light, as they were collecting some stores from Thanggu, and generously carried some of our gear for us.

We reached the foot of the Lungnak La after two hours, where I had to flee to the seclusion of the rocks, smitten again with dysentery. I looked up at the icy slope disappearing into the clouds, and wondered if I would ever make it to the top. The climb seemed interminable, although in reality it took only one hour, and it was with a sense of relief that I joined the others in the thick mist at the summit. Wangyal had seen me beginning to slow on the last steep section and had insisted on carrying my pack as well as his own up to the pass. The Lungnak

La was barren, snow covered and bitterly cold, but even there at nearly 6000m I found flowers, *Saxifraga pilifera* and its close relative *Chrysosplenium alternifolium*, growing tucked under some rocks. We paused for a while in dense mist to take some photographs, which show a group of rather haggard, cold faces. I had grown a white beard and resembled a dissipated Father Christmas with peeling nose. Altitude does nothing for your ego.

Our descent through persistent cloud and heavy rain brought us past a 200m high waterfall cascading down the north side of the valley. On one side the slope was yellow with the 2m-tall poppy *Meconopsis paniculata*, while the other slope was blue with *M.simplicifolia*. Among the rocks I found the drooping yellow flowers of *Cremanthodium reniforme*, lilac coloured *Primula deuteronana* and masses of *Primula sapphirina*, little gems with nodding blue flowers. Once again I had to suffer the frustration of a photographic ban among such a wealth of flowers.

Just before the track reached Thanggu there was an extensive grassy slope on the north side of the valley, which had a superficial resemblance to the Sussex Downs. Red and yellow flowered *Rhododendron anthopogon* took the place of hawthorn, with the small terrestrial orchids, purple *Chusua pauciflora* and green

The author on Lungnak La

Right: On the Lungnak La

Below top: Herminium josephii

Bottom: Gueldenstaedtia himalaica

Herminium josephi, interspersed with mauve trefoil-like *Gueldenstadtia himalaica* and *Aster stracheyi*. I also found *Thermopsis barbata*, a big floppy, hairy legume with purple and black flowers

Once we reached Thanggu it did not take us long to bundle all our gear into the jeeps, and set out to drive back to Gangtok. The recent heavy rain had wreaked havoc with what surface the road ever possessed, and it was after nightfall before we reached Mangan, where we were due to spend the night. No message had reached them to say that we were coming, but eventually Wangyal unearthed the chowkidar of the bungalow, and we all flopped into our sleeping bags.

We were roused the next morning by the chief inspector of police, who blessedly arrived armed with a huge flask of hot tea. As a young man he had spent a year stationed at Muguthang, and was full of stories about the area. One of our jeeps would not start, so we left Wangyal sitting on the steps of the bungalow, surrounded by bits of carburettor, while the rest of us went up to the local government offices. There we met the deputy director of agriculture and many other officials, giving us the opportunity to impress upon them the magnitude of the disaster which had befallen the farmers of Muguthang and their yak herds.

It was some months later that I learned the sequel to the story. Shortly after I left Gangtok, a deputation of senior lamas, sent by the Dalai

Lama, arrived on a fact-finding mission. Their object was to discover if any Tibetan communities were in need of help. My friends were able to tell them of the plight of the Muguthang farmers, and without more ado the elderly, but nonetheless intrepid, lamas set off over the Lungnak La to see for themselves. Financial help was promptly dispatched, and the locals came to regard our visit as heaven-sent.

We returned to the bungalow, to find Wangyal thoroughly fed up. Someone had fiddled with the jeep while we left it at Thanggu, and had not only reassembled the carburettor wrongly, but had filled the petrol tank with kerosene. Eventually he got it going, and we set off on the switchback ride to Gangtok. After all the rain, the waterfalls everywhere were an impressive sight as they thundered down to the Tista river. Flocks of swallows, crag martins and white-rumped needle-tails were milling around overhead, feeding on a recent hatch of insects, while Tibetan and black-headed shrikes were hawking over the paddyfields on a similar errand.

As we approached the teahouse by the Bakcha Chu, my friends were alarmed to see all the windows were closed and shuttered, and feared something might have happened to Grandma. To our relief we found her and half the neighbourhood gathered under an awning beside the tea-house, busy celebrating the Dalai Lama's birthday. We were warmly welcomed and given chang, most of the local farmers being already in a state of happy inebriation.

When drinking chang, ritual demands that the bamboo drinking straw is dunked up and down three times – first for religion, secondly for the local deity and thirdly for the lamas – after which it is inverted to drain out the bits of millet which get stuck in it. It is then replaced in the chang pot and serious drinking commences. The hostess tops up the pot with hot water as you drink, and protocol demands that you cannot rise from your seat until you have drained your pot. The problem was that Grandma moved like greased lightning, and took a fiendish delight in topping up my pot, so that I was in danger of being unable to rise, even if protocol were satisfied. Eventually, with a desperate effort, I drained my pot and escaped. Grandma also took Wangyal aside and, despite her small stature, proceeded to give him what sounded like a dressing down. I noticed him smirking, and when

she finally stormed off asked him what she had said. I detected a note of relish in his voice as he replied: 'I am a very naughty boy to have taken such an old man as you over the mountains!'

We reached Gangtok as darkness fell, to find the entire population apparently glued to the TV, watching Edberg and McEnroe playing at Wimbledon. It was a relief to be able to clean up properly. My hands and ankles were still badly swollen from the insect bites we had suffered days before at Lachen. Rajesh confirmed that even the local people can suffer severe reactions to the bites, with effects that last five to six days.

The next few days were spent trying to rebook flights from Bagdogra to Delhi, and onwards to London. The telephones were erratic, and all too often I would get a travel agency clerk who spoke no English. I was no more proficient in Hindi, so we

At the Bakcha Chu tea-house

Dalai Lama's birthday party

Bagdogra was chaotic. Two flights had been cancelled, and the airport was packed with angry, shouting people. It was also stiflingly hot and humid, although by then I was feeling too ill to care very much what happened. Somehow a seat on the first aircraft was found for me, another westerner and an Indian embassy official. No problem! I felt sure that we were pushed in ahead of the queue, but I was not going to argue.

The weather in Delhi was incredibly hot, and in any case I was in no mood to go sightseeing. My spirits sank to zero when I was summoned to the hotel manager's office. What could have gone wrong now? To my amazement, he and his staff were gathered to wish me a happy birthday – I had forgotten it in the midst of all the chaos, but someone must have spotted my birth date when I signed the hotel register. When I got back to my room there was a birthday cake and some fruit, with the compliments of the Hotel Siddarth. I wonder how many international hotels would measure up to that? The two room boys who arrived with cake were adamant that they were not allowed to share it. I asked, if I ordered them to sit down and have some with me, would that make it acceptable to the management? We were soon all enjoying the hotel's kindness.

rapidly reached an impasse. I was quite glad to rest up for a couple of days, as my hands and feet were now grossly swollen and resembled footballs. I spent a pleasant time in the bazaar looking for gifts to take home. I found the Sikkimese silversmiths in Gangtok particularly skilful and helpful – if you could prise them or their staff away from their TV sets: the entire population was still glued to the Wimbledon finals.

Finally the time came to say goodbye to my friends, who had entertained me so well since we returned from Thanggu. Even now the Fates had a final go at me. A lorry rammed our car on the drive down to Bagdogra, stoving in the door right beside me. We counted ourselves fortunate to be able to drive on.

Chaos ruled at Delhi airport next morning. All the passengers were sent to the wrong departure gate, so we had to endure two security checks and two X-rays. No problem! The in-flight movies were quite awful – two turgid Bollywood melodramas with lots of dancing in the most improbable locations. The only solution was to turn off the sound, making them hilarious to watch.

Back home, after what I like to think was a decent interval, my thoughts turned again to Sikkim. Memory has a remarkable capacity to block out the unpleasant features of our experiences, and the desire to get back into the remote mountains of the north of the country began to return. This time I wanted to return to Thanggu and travel north-east up the Lasha Chu to the far corner of Sikkim. Very few people, and certainly no botanists, had been there since the visit of Joseph Hooker and Dr Campbell in 1849. That made it doubly attractive.

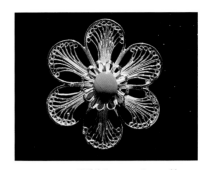

Sikkimese jewellery

In the Lal bazaar

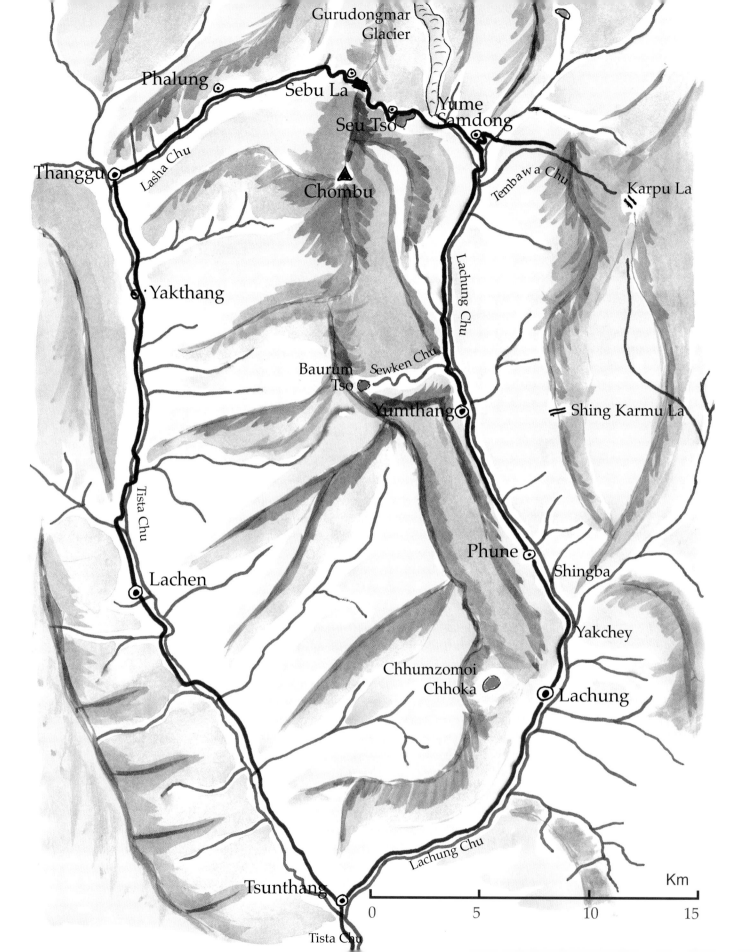

Gurudongmar
Glacier

Phalung

Sebu La

Seu Tso

Yume
Samdong

Thanggu

Lasha Chu

Chombu

Tembawa Chu

Karpu La

Lachung Chu

Yakthang

Baurum
Tso

Sewken Chu

Shing Karmu La

Yumthang

Tista Chu

Phune

Shingba

Lachen

Yakchey

Chhumzomoi
Chhoka

Lachung

Lachung Chu

Tsunthang

Tista Chu

Km

0   5   10   15

In the Steps of Hooker

*T*he next few years saw a series of emotional switchbacks in my efforts to return, and I began to fear I should never see Sikkim again . . .

Chusua puberula

Lower Chombu ice falls

There were times when another visit looked really hopeful, alternating with times of deep depression when plans collapsed and it seemed that I should never get to Sikkim again.

Others had more success. In July and August 1992 the Royal Botanic Garden Edinburgh mounted a highly successful expedition to Sikkim. The party, consisting of David Long, Ron McBeath, Henry Noltie and Mark Watson, travelled via Darjeeling to Yuksam. From there they followed the route I had covered in 1987 to Bakkhim, Tsokha, Dzongri and Thangshing, but in this case they were successful in reaching the Goecha La, and also in going from Dzongri up to Bikhbari. At the end of their stay in Gangtok they made a visit to Phodang. Some 1289 specimens of vascular plants were collected, including 21 species of *Primula* and seven of *Meconopsis*. In addition they collected 718 bryophytes and 38 lichens. The collection of flowering plants was split, and a set presented to the Botanical Survey of India in Gangtok.

After their return I wrote to David Long, suggesting the possibility of a botanical expedition in September 1995 to the Lachung valley, north to Yume Samdong and the Donkya La. I also wrote to Wangyal Tobden, to seek his opinion on the chances of an expedition to travel around Khangchendzonga on the route Hooker had followed in 1849. His reply was not encouraging. He felt, rightly as it transpired, that we should never get permission to travel north over the Donkya La. He had done the journey in the course of his police duties, and described the plateau north of Khangchengyao as cold, barren and devoid of plants except mosses. He did

suggest a more southerly route from Thanggu to Yume Samdong over the Sebu La, and it was this route which we ultimately followed. He also informed me that the American Rhododendron Society had been permitted to visit the Lachung valley, and a German party had been allowed to trek to the Zemu glacier. If we were to reach north-east Sikkim ahead of the pack we should need to get a move on.

Tashi Tobden had come to Britain on a specialist university course in 1993, and at the time felt it might indeed be possible for a botanical expedition to travel as far as Yume Samdong, but he repeated that permission to cross the Donkya La would certainly not be given. I mentioned that I was keen to follow in the steps of the renowned Joseph Hooker.

'Oh, yes,' said Tashi. 'Hooker – my great great great grandfather put him and Campbell in a dungeon. I do hope history will not repeat itself!'

The next move came in February 1994, when the Royal Botanic Garden wrote to the British High Commissioner in Delhi, Sir Nicholas Fenn, seeking his support for an expedition. At the same time letters were sent to all the relevant officials in Sikkim. In May came welcome news that the Sikkim Government approved of the expedition in principle, and had written to the Ministry of Home Affairs in Delhi. They in turn requested details of all those proposing to make the trip, and our hopes rose that we might be able to visit Sikkim in 1995 after all.

The next bombshell dropped in August 1994. In an article published in *Nature*, details emerged of new Indian legislation prohibiting the export of any animal or plant material, living or dead. Drug companies in the USA and Japan had developed medicines from plants originally collected in India, from which the Indian government gained no income. Without debating the rights and wrongs of such legislation, it effectively stopped the collection of pressed plant specimens for herbaria, an essential part of any botanical expedition. Such pressed specimens are the ultimate reference for any work on plant taxonomy in a country, and without them no worthwhile study can be undertaken.

Despite this potential stumbling block, the Royal Botanic Garden approached the Indian High Commission in London, and in January 1995 Henry Noltie and I had an amicable meeting with their staff. We were advised to submit applications for visas and the restricted area permits necessary to travel north of Gangtok. Comforting noises followed, but early in May the RBG received a letter from the Ministry of Environment and Forests in Delhi, saying that they had decided not to allow the proposed

The intended destination: Yume Samdong

expedition. A reply was sent requesting that they reconsider their decision, but effectively an expedition in 1995 was no longer possible.

To our amazement, we received a letter in August informing us that our application had been reconsidered and approved. It was all on again, and rescheduled for July 1996. In March 1996 a letter came from Usha Lachungpa, an officer with the forestry department, who had travelled extensively in north-east Sikkim over much of the route that we wished to cover. In 1995 she had gone from Thanggu over the Sebu La to Yume Samdong, and up the Tembawa Chu to the north-east. She had then doubled back and gone over the Donkya La, circling north of Khangchengyao, past the Tso Lhamo lake, returning over the Kongra La to Thanggu. Not only was this a very impressive trip, but Usha had also taken photographs of nayan, the Marco Polo sheep, and kiang, the Tibetan wild ass. She had the good fortune to obtain a picture of a mare with twin foals. It was possible that she could come with us as one of the guides, with the advantage that her husband,

Lower Tista valley

Ganden Lachungpa, ran a trekking agency in Gangtok and could arrange transport, tents and porters for us.

In mid-April Edinburgh received a letter from the forestry department in Sikkim offering help, but stating that permission to collect plant specimens must come from the Botanical Survey of India in Delhi. Another letter, from the Indian High Commission in London, stated that a letter from the Ministry of Environment and Forests, plus the normal visas, was all we needed. In the light of what happened later this was a trifle optimistic.

Final lists of personnel, dates and itinerary were now submitted to the Indian Consulate in Glasgow, which had just opened conveniently close to Edinburgh, and the British High Commission in Delhi were apprised of our plans. At the last minute we were asked to accept two Bhutanese scientists as members of our party, and two Sikkimese botanists were also to accompany us. This added to the complications, and faxes flew in all directions. In mid-June we received a letter from Dr A.S. Chauhan of BSI Gangtok offering full co- operation, and on 26th June, five days before we were due to leave, the Glasgow consulate received permission from Delhi to issue our visas and restricted area permits. No problem!

Little demons of doubt still niggled, but they were pushed to the back of our minds in the last panic-stricken moments of packing and organisation. Seven years of thinking and planning were in the balance.

On 2nd July David Long, Henry Noltie and I met at London Airport, with a large amount of excess baggage due to all the collecting gear necessary for our expedition.

KLM were not inclined to look benevolently upon us, despite official papers confirming our expedition status, and they duly charged us £480. Our journey to Delhi was uneventful, until we collected our baggage and found that the largest trunk containing all the collecting gear was missing. This was a disaster, made more aggravating by the excess baggage charge paid on it, and it could have ruined our ability to collect plant specimens. At Delhi we decided to transfer to the domestic airport, and spent the rest of a rather uncomfortable night trying to sleep on the seats. I envied my Indian fellow travellers, who seemed able to sleep soundly anywhere. Westerners seem to be the wrong shape!

Bagdogra was its usual hot and sticky self, so after waiting in vain for an hour for transport which should have been laid on, we hired a taxi for the drive to Gangtok. As in the past, pond herons, cattle egrets and great white herons dotted the rice paddies along our route, with ashy and black drongos spaced out along the telephone wires. Only the roads seemed worse than I remembered from my last visit. Soon after crossing the Tista bridge we suffered our first puncture. While the driver changed the wheel I spotted a verditer flycatcher in the trees beside us, with a noisy mixed flock of white-cheeked, red-vented and black bulbuls. At the Rongphu border post between West Bengal and Sikkim, we were kept amused, while our papers were being examined, by a pair of red-rumped swallows nesting under the eaves of the building.

Tired as we were, we were glad to reach the Tashi Delek Hotel in Gangtok, where Rajesh had arranged for us to have three adjacent rooms on a large balcony. This was essential to house the plant drying presses, which were heated by kerosene stoves, and were not the sort of things you want running all night in your bedroom in the moist heat of monsoon. Dr Chauhan, the Director of BSI Gangtok, arrived, followed by Ganden and Usha Lachungpa and their nephew Tashi. Ganden is the owner of Atlas Tours and Services, and proved both on this trip and later in 2001 to be an efficient and resourceful organiser of our travel and camping needs. The suffix -pa indicates his family origin in the village of Lachung in North Sikkim.

Lal bazaar, Gangtok

His Indian wife Usha, a strikingly pretty and vivacious woman, and an experienced wildlife officer, had travelled extensively in the more remote areas of North Sikkim. Tashi appeared deceptively stolid on first acquaintance, but proved a tower of strength and ingenuity, imbued with a wicked sense of humour. Wangyal arrived soon afterwards in great form, and all was fixed for a grand council the next day.

Problems were already rearing their ugly heads. At least two major landslides had been reported on the road between Gangtok and Tsunthang, with a severe slip, as yet unbridged, near Mangan: traffic could not get north. More serious was the fact that the home affairs ministry in Delhi had failed to notify the Sikkimese authorities or the Indian Army that we had clearance to go north, so we were stuck in Gangtok until the proper papers arrived. So much for the happy advice of the consulate in Glasgow that we had all the papers we needed.

The Lachungpas duly turned up the next morning, and we agreed the arrangements for the trek. Payment of a substantial sum in advance caused severe problems at the local bank, which ran out of cash and had to send out for more. We staggered back with huge wads of rupee notes, and would have welcomed a wheelbarrow to transport them. Then it was time to do the rounds of the various government departments who would be involved with our expedition. There still remained the problem of the lack of permission from the Ministry of Home Affairs in Delhi, where they denied all knowledge of us or our expedition. This was Indian bureaucracy at its most abysmal.

At this stage I gratefully acknowledge the great debt we owe to Tashi Tobden, Wangyal Tobden and Rajesh Lakhotia. In my innocence I had not realised their exalted status in Sikkim, knowing them firstly as good friends. They worked tirelessly, using their good offices to aid us to get the necessary papers from Delhi, telephoning and faxing ministries and the Army on our behalf. Without their help we should never have got beyond Gangtok, and would certainly never have been allowed to photograph the plants of the northern region. Few of their own scientists had been permitted to travel there, and photographic records were virtually non-existent. We were indeed privileged to have the help of such friends.

One of the promised Bhutanese botanists arrived. Sonam Wangchuk was a pleasant young man from the Bhutanese Forestry department, the idea being that he should help David and Henry with the plant collecting, and at the same time learn their methods of collecting and preserving specimens. All day the weather matched our mood – low cloud obliterated any view, and the rain fell steadily.

The 5th July dawned with thick mist, but at least the rain had temporarily stopped. Usha arrived and we drove out to the Sikkim armed police headquarters at Pangthang, where Wangyal was in charge. There he showed me some ancient firearms he had just discovered stacked away in a cupboard. To my amazement I found myself handling a pair of 'jingals', large muzzle-loaders dating from the late 19th century, of the sort used by the Tibetan army against the Younghusband expedition to Lhasa in 1904. Each gun was about 2m long, with a narrow barrel and slim, brass-bound stock. They were mounted on long, brass, two-pronged swivels, which folded back under the guns. This enabled the gunners to stand to fire the jingals. According to Wangyal the very early jingals were mounted on a pair of antelope horns. The slow-burning wicks which fired the guns were still intact, and so were the guns apart from a few wormholes in the woodwork. Sikkim possesses no national museum, and it is sad that relics such as these jingals will disintegrate from the ravages of climate and insects, with the loss of an irreplaceable part of the history of Sikkim.

Wangyal had arranged for one of his policemen to guide us up onto the forest ridge above the camp, and the little man set off at a cracking pace in the incredibly humid conditions to climb up the narrow, slippery track, with the rest of us trailing behind. I had never seen so many leeches. They were everywhere on the ground and hanging from the bushes, their heads weaving from side to side as they sought to locate us. They crawled up our boots and trousers, landed on our hats and crawled down our necks. Despite all our efforts, we got bitten many times, ending up with blood soaked shirts and socks. I do not like leeches.

Birdwatching in the high humidity and steady rain was tricky, as my spectacles and binoculars constantly misted up, but I managed to identify crowned leaf warbler, yellow-naped yuhina, strong-footed bush-warbler, Nepal sunbird, Eurasian and Himalayan cuckoos – the latter with a mournful repeated call of poo, poo-poo-poo – and the ringing calls of the great Himalayan barbet. Henry and David were happy plant hunting, but I have to admit to hating jungle. Give me the open spaces! A few orchids were in flower, *Coelogyne corymbosa* too high up in the trees

Coelogyne corymbosa

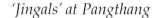

'Jingals' at Pangthang

Oberonia falcata

to photograph and an epiphyte *Oberonia falcata* with long drooping spikes of hundreds of tiny green flowers. Arisaemas flourished in the damp jungle, with some particularly fine specimens of *Arisaema tortuosum*.

Henry spent the next morning at the BSI herbarium, while the rest of us went shopping for stoves, kerosene and old newspapers for drying pressed plant specimens. In the director's office at BSI we were presented with a mass of collecting apparatus which had been left for them to use when the 1992 Edinburgh expedition to west Sikkim returned home. It had just sat there untouched, but was now an absolute godsend to us, as it replaced much of the gear which was in the missing trunk.

In the afternoon Rajesh ferried me up to the government offices at Tashiling, where I had a long meeting with the Home Department. The deputy secretary, Tsegyal Tashi, had informed the army commander of the area we hoped to visit, but the problem appeared to stem from the fact that Delhi had not notified the Sikkim Government or the military. I explained that we wished to photograph plants, so that good colour slides could accompany pressed specimens. This was met with very gloomy faces. Apparently even the Sikkim Tourist Department had not been permitted to take photographs in the northern region for the preparation of a major government report, so our own chances looked very slim. Everyone we met promised to do the best they could to help, which they most certainly did, but everything rested on the arrival of clearance papers from Delhi and the army.

When I got back to the hotel I found Sonam ill with a fever and jaundice. There was a current epidemic of infectious hepatitis in Bhutan and Sikkim, and it seemed likely that this was his problem. I felt very unhappy that he planned to accompany us to the north, since we should be nearly two weeks in very remote country and travelling at high altitude – not a good place to cope with a really sick companion. The road to Tsunthang was still not open, but messages indicated that we might be able to move north in three days time. Plans were made for Tashi Lachungpa to go ahead, to arrange porters to ferry our gear across the major landslides at the Mayan Chu and at Tung.

Insect life at the hotel was fascinating. The lights at night attracted a host of moths, including some really lovely tiger moths, and a very large beetle with antennae 8cm long and a body bearing brilliant orange spots. Sonam picked it up, and dropped it equally quickly when it emitted a very loud squeak.

Longhorn beetle

We spent a very pleasant evening with Rajesh, Wangyal and Ganden discussing our future plans. Wangyal told us that cats are cherished among the Tibetan Buddhists, because their purring is said to be their reciting of the mantra 'Om Mani Padme Hum'. Thus to kill a cat is very bad, and one would need to light one butter lamp for every hair on its body as a penance.

Next morning I went to the local hospital, to check on the results of the blood samples taken from Sonam on the previous day. The doctor I spoke to was very unhappy that he should travel in a remote area, but was also unwilling to sign any certificate to that effect, something I felt Sonam might need to present to his own department if he did not come with us.

That afternoon Rajesh drove us all down the Tista valley towards Singtam to look for wild banana – 'kaydong' – which Henry was keen to collect. From the road we could easily see the tall blade-like leaves of the banana plants growing in the steep gullies high up on the hillside, but reaching them was extraordinarily difficult. Everything was soaking wet and very slippery. David and Henry could not find the flowering spikes they needed to clarify the taxonomy of the native bananas.

These flower spikes are bizarre and impressive. More than 1m in length, they droop down with the bomb-shaped male flower at the tip, behind which are clusters of creamy coloured female flowers which develop into the 'hands' of bananas. Huge shiny purple bracts, crimson on the inside, sheathe the emerging flowers. The banana fruits they collected were small and virtually inedible, packed with large, black, very hard seeds.

That evening we were guests at the house of Tashi and Wangyal Tobden, and enjoyed a superb meal. Sikkimese food is not too fiery or overspiced for western palates, and this was simply delicious. We started with chang, which if it is well prepared has a clean tang with a hint of apples about it. Many dishes were served, including bamboo shoots, momus (the spicy dumplings I had already met in Bhutan), roast pork, a local type of spinach, rice, chicken and vegetables. Among the latter was a very large and delicious cucumber, very sweet to the taste. To make our evening even better, permits had arrived for us to make a trip the next day to Changu Lake (Tsomgo Tso) on the road east of Gangtok to the Natu La, bordering the Chumbi valley.

A taxi arrived next morning to take us to Changu, but it soon proved a lethal mix of bald tyres, faulty brakes and a dangerously incompetent driver. After a great many protestations a jeep was found, as we had

Mani wall

Left to right:
Primula reticulata,
Bhutanthera albomarginata
and Iris clarkei

originally requested, and with it a delightful driver, the antithesis of the madman we had originally suffered. The road, which goes beyond Changu to the Natu La and from there to the Chumbi valley, is an endless series of hairpin bends, with frequent landslips and appalling surfaces. No one should ever attempt to do the journey in a taxi – a jeep is essential. We chugged on in pouring rain and thick mist, past endless depressing army camps and road menders' shacks.

The surrounding hills, which in Hooker's time were covered in magnificent forest, are alas now bald and eroded. The view was mercifully shrouded in mist, but we did glimpse a few birds through the murk, among them black-faced laughing-thrush, white-capped and black redstarts, ravens and rufous-backed accentors.

The lake itself was a great disappointment, a really dreary place of black waters surrounded by black cliffs, the stony shore ringed on the north side with army sheds and dozens of scruffy tea-stalls. The surrounding hills were suffering from severe overgrazing by yaks, but still contained some good plants. By now we were very short of time, so we were unable to stray far from the road, yet we recorded masses of *Primula sikkimensis* and its close relative *P.reticulata* with paler, drooping flowers and net-veined leaves. Several terrestrial orchids grew on the roadside, purple *Chusua pauciflora*, the little musk orchid *Herminium macrophyllum* and a charming little orchid *Bhutanthera albomarginata*. This had a flower spike about 6cm tall emerging from a single clasping leaf, the blue-green flowers, white-edged and covered in white hairs, looking as if they had been frosted. All the slopes were covered in *Iris clarkei*, a fine iris with deep purple falls flecked with gold.

Our driver was getting nervous, as the rain had intensified and the clouds darkened, and he feared that some sections of the road might have become impassable. We set off back to Gangtok, passing plenty of tall *Meconopsis paniculata* and the smaller *Cathcartia villosa* with drooping yellow flowers. I had hoped to stop to photograph these, but the light was abysmal, and anyway 'We are bound to see masses of it elsewhere'. We never saw it again!

The drive down was hair-raising. Extensive landslides had to be negotiated, the jeep barely scraping over the debris, and at times skirting muddy, crumbly edges above sheer drops: not a drive for the faint hearted.

Back at the hotel we found that there was still a problem with our permits. Delhi was denying all knowledge of us. We also had to go into town to get extra photographs for police permits, the results of which can only serve to confirm police suspicions that you all look like terrorists or criminals.

The next day 'dawned' with a thick, dripping mist: no view. We were all getting depressed and frustrated, with a whole week passed and our departure no nearer. Tashi had personally telephoned the Home Affairs Ministry in Delhi, to be told they had no papers about us. Faxes flew between Gangtok, Edinburgh and Glasgow. When our original permission came it was from the Ministry of Environment and Forests, who in turn said that they were seeking approval from the Home Affairs Ministry. When in August 1995 they gave permission,

The road near Bitu

Hoya acuminata

we all assumed that the ministry had approved. In January, when we re-applied, we were told that the permission still held good, since the relevant passage told us that 'Team is welcome to visit Sikkim for field observations – BSI should be contacted'. Finally, at 7pm, Tashi telephoned to say that government and army permits were all promised by fax the next day. This was followed by a call from Glasgow, confirming that Delhi did know about us and had given permission. The convolutions of the whole business were almost beyond belief, but plans were now made to depart on 11th July.

We spent the next day on a drive out along the North Sikkim Highway towards the Bakcha Chu, as this would not involve crossing any check points. We stopped frequently to botanise along the roadsides, especially where steep cliffs and waterfalls overhung the road. I was intrigued by the name of one bridge, which was called Bitu. I assumed that this was a dialect name, but it apparently derived from the numbering of the bridges by the engineers: this was Bridge no. B2! There along the foot of the cliff small yellow *Mimulus nepalensis* grew in profusion, and on the cliff flowered the little ginger *Caulokaempferia sikkimensis*, with rosettes of crinkly leaves and pink and white flowers. Most beautiful of all were the flowers of *Hoya acuminata*, pink centred white flowers with long pointed petals, looking as if they were made of sugar icing.

I walked ahead to birdwatch, leaving my friends busy collecting plant specimens, and was rewarded by golden and black eagles, white-throated yuhinas, the very pretty white-tailed nuthatch, ashy drongos, great hill barbets and black-capped sibias in the treetops, all singing fit to burst. Up on a cliff above the road I could see a nice clump of *Chlorophytum nepalense* with flowers like white stars, and climbed up to get a specimen. Everything was very wet, and before I knew what had happened my feet flew out into thin air and I dropped 5m down onto the road. After some time I collected my wits, and realised that, apart from having cut and bruised legs, I had broken my left forearm and dislocated a bone in my wrist. At that stage things had not started to hurt too badly, so I hit the wrist smartly, and the dislocation shot back into place. I then made my way back to the jeep, and was glad to sit down. What worried me most was the prospect of not being able to continue with the expedition. This was a Colles fracture, not a clean break, so there was a good chance that if I could strap it up sufficiently, I should be able to manage reasonably well.

We drove to the teahouse at the Bakcha Chu, where I received a warm welcome from Ama Tshering. Grandma was in great form, and looked unchanged by the passing years. On the wall I was delighted to see the colour photographs of the family which I had sent them after my first visit. The grandchildren had both grown up a lot, but sadly the little boy had a foot amputated and was walking on crutches. My limited command of the language did not enable me to find out what had happened. Our return to Gangtok took place in torrential rain. At the Rate Chu we had to wait for them to blast and bulldoze clear another landslip. Back at the hotel I strapped my wrist firmly, and downed some aspirin.

Tashi arrived, smiling broadly, with some of our permits. Due to restrictions and the state of the roads it was advised that we go first to the Lachung valley, then return to Tsunthang before going north to Thanggu. We hoped then to cross the Sebu La as planned, and return straight back from Yume Samdong.

11th of July, my birthday. Up at 5.30am, with the wonderful prospect of getting on our way, the best present I could have received. My arm was still very painful, but a little less swollen, and I could just move my fingers. Simple jobs, like doing up buttons and zips, took ages and were really difficult. We were on the road by 7.15am, our two jeeps tightly packed with gear and bodies, and everything on the roof secured under tarpaulins. The rain fell in bucketloads.

Soon after Mangan we met the first big break in the road at the Meyong Chu. A huge landslide more than 100m wide had carried away both the bridge and the road, and through the gap the water poured in a raging torrent. We had to climb up a very steep temporary path above the slide and cross on an even more temporary suspension bridge of slats. We abandoned our jeeps and walked on about 4km to just short of Tung, where we met with a second and even larger landslip. Here a really massive slide had carried away a big bridge and all the approach roads. Bulldozers had carved a steep zigzag approach out of the hillside to the crossing. It was rather like driving down the side of a badly maintained quarry. Army engineers were busy erecting a bailey bridge, and had progressed so well that we were able to walk over it, although it was not secure enough for vehicles to cross.

We waited for ages in the rain for Tashi Lachungpa to find two jeeps to carry us to Tsunthang, and for porters to arrive with all our gear carried on from the Meyong Chu. At every obstruction there would always be a group of porters patiently waiting for you to hire them to carry your gear across the slide. This was a porters' market, and one was forced to accept the going rate for the job, however high it might be. While we waited, we watched five army trucks being driven through the torrent above the remains of the bridge. They made an impressive picture, like big green elephants wading a river, the water nearly reaching into the high cabs. Then some local traders, laden with cabbages and unwilling to wait for the bridge to be completed, decided to take their smaller lorries through. Inevitably the first one got stuck and stalled in mid-torrent, with water pouring through the cab. They climbed forlornly on top of the cabbages to get out of the water. At that stage we were forced to leave the drama, which the locals were thoroughly enjoying, as our jeeps had arrived to take us on to Tsunthang.

Didymocarpus oblongus

Waterfall near Tsungta

The road from Tung was an endless series of bends, vertiginous edges, cloud and rain. The Tista Chu from Mangan northwards gets more and more impressive, especially just below Tsunthang, where the road crosses to the west bank by a new bridge beside the old suspension bridge. The river far below was a foaming, roaring maelstrom. Further north the river runs in a deep gorge, and at the confluence of the Tista and the Lachung Chu it is a wonderful sight, with the Tista almost out of view in its deep gorge. Birdwatching from the jeep was hopeless, although I did spot a large, pale eagle sitting wet and miserable in a tree top in the mist.

We reached Tsunthang without problem, and soon settled into the comfortable dak bungalow, spreading all our gear out to dry. Our group was a most agreeable one, consisting of Henry Noltie and David Long, professional and highly competent botanists from the Royal Botanic Garden Edinburgh, Dr Sinha from BSI Gangtok, a kindly, bearded lichenologist, Sonam Wangchuk from Bhutan, Usha Lachungpa, whose speciality was the study of mammals and birds, Lakhpa Tsering our mountaineering specialist, a delightful, courteous and very tough character, Tashi Lachungpa who was proving highly efficient and a wizard at organisation, and, by no means least, our cook Suren Sunar, who throughout the trek produced excellent food under difficult conditions.

Next morning I was in trouble, and found many simple tasks impossible single-handed. David zipped up my trek bag, while Sonam stuffed my sleeping bag back into its container. We were lucky to have reached Tsunthang when we did, as some huge boulders had come crashing down in the night, and completely blocked the road behind us. In Hooker's day Tsunthang consisted of a gompa and twenty houses. Now it is a busy small town, pleasantly situated at the confluence of the Tista and the Lachung Chu, with steep forested slopes rising on all sides. Tsunthang means 'the meadow of marriage', and relates to the meeting of the two rivers. We set off up the Lachung road, with steep cliffs on one side, and on the other a precipitous drop to the foaming, thundering river. The waterfalls were absolutely lovely, and at Tsungta a bridal-veil fall crashed down hundreds of metres to a roadside pool.

We were not in a great hurry, and every time we stopped to admire the view or look at plants we also saw plenty of birds, common hawk-cuckoos, pied chats, black-capped sibias, white-tailed nuthatches and a streaked spider-hunter, a thrush sized bird with broad wings and a whopping great curved bill like a mini-curlew. On the rocks above the road were the big round leaves of *Bergenia purpurescens*, mauve *Roscoea purpurea* and the drooping pink flowers of the orchid *Anthogonium gracile*. Just below Lachung the valley starts to open out, and here the farmers were growing cabbages intensively, a new venture. It was one of their lorries which stuck in the flood at Tung. On a large boulder we could see a gorgeous clump of the orchid *Pholidota recurva*, with masse of orange-throated cream flowers, but it was completely out of reach. However, a kindly farmer saw our plight and fetched a ladder so that we could reach and photograph it.

On the opposite side of the valley the *Tsuga dumosa* forest was magnificent, with trees growing right up the sides of the towering cliffs. Hooker describes Lachung as a village of one hundred wooden houses raised on posts. This style persists, since the sides of the valley are so steep that any house built level with the road has to be supported by stilts as the ground drops away. The dark timber frames, infilled with white painted boards and topped with wide wooden shingled roofs, reminded me strongly of the houses in Bhutan. The space underneath each house was used for storing materials such as timber and fodder.

At Lachung we met our first army check-post, where we were ordered to the side of the road, and Usha departed with all our papers and permits. Despite her charm, everything was going very slowly, as every form was minutely examined, until the brigadier arrived – a delightful and courteous man. Immediately everyone became super-efficient! He was well acquainted with us and our problems, and we were soon happily on our way. For the first time since we arrived in Sikkim I began to think that we might actually reach the north, and do what we had set out to do.

Above Lachung the road was good but twisty, and, as we climbed, the forest gradually improved, showing some evidence of regeneration. The roadsides were a mass of purple *Roscoea purpurea* and some small green orchids not identifiable from a moving jeep. In the mist we could see the tall white spires of the giant lily *Cardiocrinum giganteum* high up on the sides of the valley.

Finally we reached the Phune rest-house in the Shingba rhododendron reserve. This was small but well built, and very clean with a broad verandah. The porters soon

Pholidota recurva

Cardiocrinum giganteum

Phune Lodge, Shingba

had a fire going, but it smoked so badly that we were nearly stifled and had to put it out. The chowkidar had a ginger and white cat, which lived with a small black and very friendly puppy. They soon decided it would be more fun to move in with us – better than being stuck in a kennel.

A brief walk along the road, during one of the few breaks in the rain, brought us a tall, purple flowered *Corydalis*, *Tofieldia himalaica* and graceful sprays of *Streptopus simplex* on the moss covered rocks. In the garden around the hut we saw black-faced laughing-thrushes and whistling thrushes, while a flock of Nepal rosefinches were feeding where the puppy had spilt a bowl of rice. As darkness fell a roding woodcock flew past through the trees. The Shingba Forest around Phune was lovely, despite quite extensive and illegal tree felling by local people. Much of the original forest remained, stretching from the shingly banks of the Lachung Chu up to the flanks of steep, jagged mountains, down which cascaded hundreds of waterfalls. Low cloud and rain obliterated the view for most of our stay, but we had tantalising glimpses of sparkling snow peaks above dark cliffs.

Before breakfast next morning we walked down into the forest and found it good for birds, Pallas's warbler, white-collared blackbird, whistling thrush wherever there was running water, plain-backed mountain-thrush singing short mellow phrases from the treetops, rufous-bellied woodpecker and a small flock of imperial pigeons. They looked huge in the dim forest light, with grey heads and dark backs.

We were permitted at this stage to go as far north as Yumthang, where there was another dak bungalow and a few shacks on the edge of very heavily grazed meadows. The valley there was wide and flat, and the Lachung Chu ran in numerous channels between gravel banks. Common sandpipers and large pied wagtails were nesting, but more exciting were two pairs of ibisbill, each pair with a large downy chick. Ibisbill are one of my favourite birds, not least for their habit of nesting in remote, high altitude river valleys. About the size of a small curlew, they are steel grey in colour with a white belly contrasting sharply with a black band across the lower breast, black cap and chin. The beak is curved like that of a curlew, but it and the legs are bright coral red in colour. Despite this bold pattern, ibisbill are past masters of camouflage. You can watch them fly in to a gravel bank right in front of you, where they will instantly disappear from view. These birds were more obliging, since they were keeping a watchful eye on their very active offspring. When they moved they ran partly crouched, with the beak stretched out along the ground as if to reduce their silhouette. The meadows and river bank at Yumtang were full of colour, blue *Chesneya nubigena*, yellow potentillas, several species of bright pink *Pedicularis*, and hundreds of small green terrestrial orchids of four genera – *Platanthera*, *Listera*, *Herminium* and *Malaxis*.

We retreated to the rest house to eat our picnic lunches under cover, as the rain sluiced down. There we also met three forestry department staff who had been assigned to our party, and seemed bent on billeting themselves on our already cramped quarters at Phune. They were soon told by our staff that it simply would not do, but they did not endear themselves to us by

their aggressive attitude, and we learned with sinking hearts that they intended to accompany us over the Sebu La.

We decided to walk back to Phune, despite the weather. Our route back took us down to the edge of the Lachung Chu, which was in full spate. A cantilevered stone bridge had been built out to mid-stream, but efforts to span the entire river had failed. There was evidence of severe flood damage all along the valley. In 1994 a massive landslide north of Yume Samdong in the Tembawa Chu valley destroyed a glacial moraine dam retaining a large lake. This promptly emptied in a devastating flood, which wiped out every low-level bridge for 185km downstream all the way to

Ibisbill [Nigel Tucker/ Nature Picture Library]

Shingba Forest Reserve

Aorchis spathulata

A bridge too far: Lachung Chu

the plains of Bengal. Surprisingly, nobody was killed. (We were later to visit the site of the empty lake at the end of our trek.) In the forest we saw a few more birds we had not seen before: chough, great tit, crowned leaf-warbler, Sikkim tree-creeper and red-headed bullfinch. The females of this last species are extremely attractive, having an all-gold head, black face mask and grey back.

The black puppy was now firmly attached to Henry. It was a dear little thing, but somewhat noisy. Our cook had taken a great deal of trouble over the evening meal, which was superb. We even had a menu carefully written out:

1 *Vegetable Manistory Soup*
2 *Vegetable Chow Mein*
3 *Desert Strawberry Stream Lemon*

Good cooks are to be treasured, especially on trek. Ours was not only a good cook, but delightful company as well.

All night long the rain poured down. At dawn a small flock of very wet rosefinches were back at their task of clearing up the puppy's leftover rice. We decided to walk down through the forest back towards

Lachung, leaving the jeep to follow later in the day to bring us back.

Before long we stopped to admire a large colony of *Aorchis spathulata* growing on top of a moss covered rock, delightful purple orchids with dark spotted lips. Right beside them grew a large clump of *Pleione hookeriana*, sadly a bit worse for wear from the foul weather. The flowers were large, with white perianth segments and a lip spotted with mauve and yellow.

The edge of the forest was reached, with open grassy country where I found the small pink orchid *Gymnadenia orchidis*, much like a pale version of our own Fragrant Orchid. The road then descended in a series of tight hairpins, so we cut straight down the hillside along a stream gully which looked interesting. Through wet-misted spectacles, I saw what at first I took to be a colony of alpine butterwort on a very wet bank above the stream. On closer inspection I found they were tiny orchid flowers set on delicate stems, with linear leaves like grass. Henry promptly identified them as *Chusua puberula*. The flowers were pure white, with a broad lip divided into two arms and legs, the centre of the lip marked with vermilion spots. The sepals and upper petals formed a small hood striped with red, the whole flower resembling a tiny Lady Orchid.

Further on we found the road blocked by a raging torrent. One of our forestry department companions, the slightly portly Gut, tried to be dashing and leaped across, landing firmly in the deepest bit and getting extremely wet. At that moment our jeep arrived and ferried the rest of us across in the dry. I had never seen Dr Sinha laugh so much before.

Lachung valley

We drove down to Yakchey, just uphill from the village of Lachung, where there was a tourist lodge. The decor was a trifle weird, but at least we were able to eat our lunch under cover. The fields around Yakchey proved very interesting, David and Henry collecting a wealth of specimens. I walked on a little further, past road verges bright with masses of purple flowered *Roscoea purpurea*. In a wet gully I found a single tree of *Magnolia globosa*, which had been lopped and severely mangled, but a side branch bore some gorgeous big white flowers with broad waxy petals, and a strong fragrance. In the same gully I found a single spike of the small cobra lily *Arisaema echinatum*. This was a real gem of a plant, with a virtually stemless hooded flower some 8cm tall, striped with purplish brown. The spadix was dark and bristly and the spathe ended in a sharp point. This species had not previously been recorded in Sikkim. On our way back to Phune we could see several stands of the giant lily

Arisaema echinatum

Cardiocrinum giganteum lurking in the mist, high up on the side of the valley. I also discovered I had collected a good company of leeches, which had got inside my shirt and gorged themselves.

The road between Lachung and Tsunthang was blocked by yet another landslide, so it was to everyone's surprise and delight that Ganden Lachungpa arrived at the lodge at 6pm, having walked across the slide, bringing with him all the necessary permits we required for our journey to Thanggu and the Sebu La. It was very good to see him.

That evening the Gut made a very odd statement to me: 'You were in army'. I was amazed, since my only experience had been as a national serviceman in 1953, and a very short experience it had proved to be. There was something reminiscent of Spike Milligan and the Goons in 22922676 Gunner Lang being seen as a threat to Indian security, considering that I had been thrown out of the army after two months for being so short sighted as to constitute a threat to my own side if ever let loose with a gun!

The following morning Sonam was a sad sight, with his face and eyelids swollen up and with severe conjunctivitis. The possible cause was an allergy triggered by handling the plant material we had collected, probably one of the Euphorbia, so I treated him with antihistamines and eye ointment.

We went down again towards Lachung in a thick blanket of mist to where the road descends steeply, where we crossed a small river and climbed up a horrendously steep jungly slope. I could see some superb Cardiocrinum giganteum high above me, and after many slips and falls I reached them, to find that the flowers still towered high above my head making photography very difficult. They had the most gorgeous scent, which was still detectable 5m away. We also found Rhododendron camelliiflorum in flower, but in an unreachable position high on a cliff. Further down towards the village we found a fine stand of Cardiocrinum in flower right beside the road. Crossing the Lachung Chu by the bridge in the village, we walked along the south bank of the river for some way on a forest track. The river was an impressive sight, thundering down in full spate.

By evening Sonam was feeling extremely unwell, and the decision was made that he would leave us at Tsunthang before we went north, and return to Bhutan to recover. Just for once we awoke to a gloriously sunny morning, with the peaks and glaciers north of Yume Samdong glittering white beneath a blue sky. Behind the bungalow the sheer rockfaces soared up to spiky peaks. There was little time to enjoy our surroundings, however, as we packed all our

New gompa at Lachen

gear into a jeep and a small truck for the journey to Lachen. In Tsunthang we bade farewell to Sonam, and set off at last up the Tista valley. We stopped briefly to look for plants on an overhanging rock face beside the road, where we found yellow *Viola wallichiana*, and a delicate twining plant with tubular blue flowers, *Leptacodon gracile*. While I waited for the others, I watched a large juvenile eagle hotly pursued by a mob of drongos, a single verditer flycatcher and a brilliantly coloured male scarlet finch.

Just short of Lachen we stopped to look for the blue *Hydrangea stylosa*, which I had found in pouring rain and semi-darkness in 1989. While I was photographing it, the Brigadier passed in his staff car. Usha was invited up to the camp to see him, and returned very satisfied with his promise to help if we had any problems.

The last section of the road between Tsunthang and Lachen is very impressive. The Tista Chu runs deep down in a sheer-sided gorge, spanned by a remarkable suspension bridge with a vast drop below it. We crossed several minor landslides and chugged through several deep streams flooding across the road, but we had no serious problems. We were accommodated in the same dak bungalow where I had stayed in 1989. It was by far the best we had experienced, and was much nicer than my jaundiced memory of staying there with Wangyal, Rajesh and Lekshed, when I had been so badly smitten with claustrophobia. No problem this time!

We had made such good time on our drive that I was able to get out after lunch and walk up the hillside above the village with our mountain guide Lakhpa Tsering. He set off at a cracking pace, past the very

smart new gompa, the woodwork gleaming with red, blue and gold, which had been built since my last visit to replace the old gompa. The huge rose bush, which had been such a feature, had been cleared away. The hillside was heavily grazed, and I was unable to find the tree covered in *Pleiones* which I remembered so vividly. At least this time we could wander at will, with no armed escort trailing behind us. The slender, drooping pink flowers of *Anthiogonum gracile* were plentiful on rock outcrops out of reach of the ubiquitous yaks, but what thrilled me most was a small patch of the orchid *Spathoglottis ixioides*, the flowers a brilliant deep yellow, which shone despite the torrential rain. Lakhpa and I squelched back downhill, through scrub crawling with leeches. I thought that I had avoided their attentions, but later found three large fat ones under my blood-soaked shirt.

In the bungalow a fire was lit, and we were able to relax in comfortable chairs, the first we had sat in for some days, and write up our journals by candlelight: all very civilised. We discovered that our onward journey would be with different vehicles and drivers. The local mafia would not let our Gangtok drivers on their stretch of road, so we had to employ them, at an inflated rate of course. My recollections of Lachen village were fairly accurate. It really was a rather grotty, muddy place, with uninspired architecture apart from the new gompa and a fine three-storey house at the north end of the village. It had an air of a place permanently set under a depression. I felt that little had changed since Hooker was there on his way up the Zemu Chu to the Lhonak valley in July 147 years earlier. Even the weather was the same – wet.

Riverside flowers, Yumthang

129

Meconopsis paniculata

Above right: Rhododendron lepidotum

Tsoptha, Thanggu

The night that followed could most kindly be described as disturbed. My hand swelled up so that my fingers resembled sausages, and ached abominably. Beds were in short supply, so some of us slept on the floor. Dr Sinha snored so loudly that I swear the floorboards vibrated in sympathy. Poking him at regular intervals was only partly successful.

Next day we reached Thanggu in barely two hours' driving, setting up our gear in the very adequate bungalow, where our porters soon had a good fire going and coffee brewed. The bungalow was situated at the north end of the village on a rise below the small gompa, commanding good views across the valley past Hooker's Rock – the huge glacial erratic boulder that I remembered from my last visit.

Henry had noticed some interesting country just before we reached the village, so we went back for several kilometres to a rocky plateau above the river, where we found the 2m tall spires of *Meconopsis paniculata* covered in big pale yellow flowers, blue *M.simplicifolia*, two orchids *Chusua pauciflora* and *Gymnadenia orchidis*, and the big peony-like flowers of *Podophyllum emodi*. The latter is a protected species, since it and some close relatives are the source of some interesting alkaloids whose use in the treatment of various cancers is currently under evaluation. The plant has big lobed leaves and large drooping white flowers. The slopes above the road were covered in dwarf *Rhododendron lepidotum* in full flower, the three forms of mauve, pink and yellow making a fine splash of colour.

When I had previously stayed at Thanggu, I had looked longingly at the slopes across the valley which I had only been able to visit so briefly before I was stopped by the military. The area is called Tsoptah, and consists of big rocky outcrops, closely grazed terraces and small bright green areas of bog, fed by little streams and full of yellow *Pedicularis longiflora*. This time we were able to spend the afternoon there, accompanied by our forestry department helpers, and – to do them justice – they proved to have sharp eyes for spotting interesting plants and genuinely seemed to enjoy themselves.

It proved to be a splendid site for the smaller terrestrial orchids, with many musk orchids *Herminium josephi*, a small green *Platanthera*, a delightful yellow green *Habenaria diphylla* with a lip divided into three long appendages and, tucked under the juniper bushes, small clumps of *Malaxis muscifera* with big shiny leaves and spikes of tiny green flowers. The small purple orchids *Chusua pauciflora* and *Aorchis spathulata*, which we had previously seen at Phune, here grew in profusion, and scattered in the short turf were several species of minute, bright blue annual gentians.

I was unable to locate the site where I had previously found *Cypripedium himalaicum*, although in retrospect I think we were about 1km too far north, but one could spend many happy hours pottering about the whole valley if time would permit. We then scrambled down towards the valley floor, finding *Gymnadenia orchidis* in quantity, and a single spike of *Neottianthe secundiflora*, the

Thanggu gompa

Left: Habenaria diphylla var.josephii

Meconopsis simplicifolia

deep magenta flowers bearing a stout spur and round lip, with two small side lobes darker in colour.

Hooker remarked in his journal on the abundance of *Primula sikkimensis* in the marshy fields at Thanggu, and we, too, found fields yellow with thousands of flowers. Both the flowers and

the rather bushy leaves appear to be unpalatable, since the grazing animals had not touched them.

Later in the day I paid a visit to the little gompa above our camp. Alongside the path stood a line of Tibetan style stupas, alternate ones painted white or orange, with a tall line of prayer flags waving in the wind. From the terrace of the gompa I could look west up the valley towards the Lungnak La which I had crossed in 1989 to the Lhonak valley. The gompa was of very simple design, looked after by a single, young, very hospitable lama. He invited me in to take butter tea, and we struggled to understand each other in Gurkhali – the only language we had in common.

The evening turned out fine, with clear skies. Across the valley I could see squadrons of giant rhubarb marching up the steep mountain sides, and our hopes rose for an improvement in the weather.

18th July dawned misty and dry, but not for long. At last we were off on a trek that

Getting ready to leave Thanggu

*Below right:
Primula sikkimensis at Thanggu*

Lilium nanum

expression on either side. We kept this up throughout the trip, to the delight of the other porters, until the last day, when he wrung my hand, grinning from ear to ear.

Hooker left Thanggu in May 1849, and walked up the Lasha Chu valley to an area known nowadays as Phalung. We followed in his footsteps, up past the gompa and eastwards up a good track above the river – a steady trudge. The flowers along the path were a constant delight, especially the profusion of small orchids which included many we had seen at Tsoptah, *Habenaria diphylla*, *Gymnadenia orchidis*, *Herminium josephi* and the musk orchid I knew so well from the Sussex Downs, *Herminium monorchis*. Other plants of interest were *Lilium nanum* in its yellow flowered form, the snakeshead *Fritillaria cirrhosa*, and the two blue poppies *Meconopsis simplicifolia* and the beautiful ice blue *M. horridula*. This is certainly one of my favourite flowers, despite the name it has earned by the wealth of golden bristles which cover the leaves and stems. In one dry gully I found an *Onosma* with bristly leaves and drooping, wine-red flowers, and cushions of an *Arenaria* with big creamy flowers, accompanied by its relative *A. melandryoides* with flowers of a striking pink colour.

for seven years had been a tantalising dream. Outside the bungalow, Tashi was busy organising the porters with almost military precision, as loads were checked and divided to make them as even as possible. I had hoped that we would be using yaks for the journey, but we were told very clearly that the route was only feasible using human porters: this proved correct.

Among the porters was one older man, a little bit older than me, but about three times older than the others. Despite his age he carried as much or more than anyone else, and was always at the head of the party. His face was wrinkled and totally impassive, giving a completely misleading impression of severity, belied by his ability to reduce all around him to tears of mirth with a few words. I discovered that we were both grandfathers, so each morning we would bow and address each other with 'Good morning, revered grandfather!' This was delivered without a flicker of

Despite the now constant drizzle and low cloud, we saw flocks of hill and snow pigeons, alpine choughs and pink-browed rosefinches, with the occasional Hodgson's tree-pipit running about on the grass, and a single raven soaring overhead. The path climbed steadily, leaving the river far below, and we passed through a zone of dwarf rhododendrons where clumps of *Androsaces* and *Saxifrages* grew in every rock cleft. Our path branched northwards to the camp site at Lasha, but away to the east the valley of the Lasha Chu was an amazing sight. The valley floor is perfectly flat and wide for miles, bounded by steep mountains on either side, while the river forms the most perfect series of meanders, ox-bows and cut-offs I have ever seen – a sight to delight any student of geomorphology. Hooker was also enchanted by them.

Lasha is a place of wide open, windy grass slopes, across which the rain drove with evil persistence, so that we were glad to find that our good porters had pitched all the tents by the time of our arrival. Around the camp Hume's groundpeckers hopped, accompanied by youngsters scarcely able to fly, with Blyth's pipits, orange-breasted robin accentors and dowdy Hodgson's mountain finches creeping around like little mice. Usha had seen Himalayan snowcock on her previous visit to the area, but despite getting up at dawn when they are supposed to be most vocal, and straining my ears to the mists, I never heard a single cackle.

Usha and I were up early to search for snowcock on the slopes above our camp. She had stayed overnight with relatives in a small stone hut on the mountainside, where we called in and were entertained with Tibetan tea. Usha's uncle was a delightful

man with a round beaming face, and pigtails braided in a circle behind his head. He always appeared immaculately dressed in white silk shirt, and baggy black trousers tucked into polished boots. The interior of the house was similarly immaculate, with beautiful carpets and gleaming butter lamps set before statues of the Buddha. Over tea he told us that one of the yaks had given birth overnight, but unfortunately the calf had been killed by ravens. The new-born yak calves were small and vulnerable, with an average birth weight of 20kg.

While we drank our tea, one of the farmer's sons was busy dressing up their best yak and himself in all their finery for a special festival and yak races to be held later that day at Phalung. The festival of Drukpa Tseshi celebrates the first teaching of the Buddha, and gives an opportunity for all the local herdsmen and their families to gather together for ceremonies to bless the yaks, and afterwards enjoy a feast, dances and yak races. Usha and Ganden had told us beforehand of the festival at Phalung, and it was a happy circumstance that brought us there at just the right time. Phalung, which Hooker called Palung, is a wide open area of heavily grazed yak pasture, with great mountains soaring skywards to the north. The latter was something we had to take on trust, as we were literally at cloud base level, and could see nothing. Dotted over the pastures were the summer tents of the yak herders. These

Alpine chough [Jose B. Ruiz/ Nature Picture Library]

Robin accentor

Onosma aff.hookeri

133

A DAY IN YAK COUNTRY

Clockwise from above: Lama performing puja; the winner of the yak races; yak herders' huts, Phalung; yak dressed for Drukpa Tseshi

were made of woven squares of black yak hair, joined together and stretched over a frame set in a rectangle of stone blocks. The stone walls remain from season to season, the tents being taken down at the end of the grazing season in October. The fabric looks coarse, but is very waterproof, since when it rains the damp fibres swell, making the weave even tighter.

The yaks were a wonderful sight, with red, blue and yellow tassels and balls of wool plaited into their tails and hung from their horns. Their halters and face bands were decorated with patterns of cowrie shells and hung with little brass bells, while the saddles were covered in richly coloured pieces of carpet. The effect was slightly marred by matted hair and mud, since no one had thought to groom them first. One special yak was led up to the puja ceremony, finely dressed and sporting an auspiciously white tail.

We were anxious not to intrude on the puja, but our hosts insisted that we join in, and ushered us into the main stone building, where a lama from the Lachen gompa was preparing the rites. To my surprise, he and the elders were quite happy for us to take photographs. The lama sat behind a small table, on which he had placed his scriptural texts bound between two wooden blocks, cymbals and dorji. On a stand beside him was an upright drum, brightly painted in swirling patterns of blue and gold. This he struck at regular intervals with a long, curved stick. Behind him in an alcove were dozens of butter lamps, silver bowls piled with rice, and above them brightly painted butter sculptures of discs and geometric shapes coloured red and green. In front of him a large tin bath was

filled with offerings of cheese, money and, strangely enough, packets of Cornish wafer biscuits.

There followed a long period of chants, alternating with crescendoes of drumming and clashing of cymbals. Outside an acolyte, smartly clad in a black robe with broad blue cuffs and a bright red sash, his head topped with a fur-trimmed gold hat, had lit a smoking fire of juniper wood. As each crescendo of chanting and drumming reached a peak, he dipped a ladle into a pan of boiled rice and threw it high in the air, presumably as an offering to the gods.

Next came the yak races, eagerly anticipated by the locals, who almost certainly had bets laid on favoured beasts and jockeys. The field was small, as yak herds had been decimated during the previous winter by severe weather. The four runners lined up tidily enough, but then all semblance of order was lost as the entrants galloped off in all directions, egged on by the cheering onlookers, their riders vainly trying to steer them along the chosen race course. The whole set-up reminded me of a small local point-to-point, so much more fun than the beautifully arranged big events. Our farmer friend's son came in miles ahead of all the others, and was duly given his prize money and draped with a ceremonial scarf by the lama. David and I were then induced to mount yaks and have our photographs taken, looking as self-conscious as children set on camels at a zoo.

The marshy fields around Phalung proved excellent for flowers, despite their overgrazed appearance. I particularly relished two saxifrages we found growing along the edges of little runnels of icy cold water. *Saxifraga cordigera* bore single, very

Saxifraga melanocentra

Saxifraga cordigera

large, drooping yellow flowers, the whole calyx, stem and leaves being thickly covered with dark red, glistening hairs. *Saxifraga melanocentra* was even more bizarre, with chocolate coloured stigmas in the centre of big white petals, each bearing a yellow patch, surrounded in turn by a scarlet calyx – a saxifrage which looked as if it had been designed by Walt Disney. The little pink *Primula tibetica* that I remembered from Muguthang also grew here in profusion, with the larger flowered mauve *P.primulina*, which has each flower's throat packed with tiny white hairs.

In the afternoon, with two of the porters who were showing a great interest in plant collecting, we scrambled down the steep hillside to the meanders of the Lasha Chu. There we spent a happy time, finding many plants we had not recorded before. Among them was a member of the campanula family, *Codonopsis foetans*, with very large pale blue, drooping bellflowers borne singly on wiry stems, each bell exquisitely marked

Meanders,
Upper Lasha Chu

on the inside with purple veins. What was not quite so exquisite was the fox-like smell, which gave it its name.

That night our cook, Suren Sunar, excelled himself. Supper consisted of a fine vegetable soup laced with fresh ginger, slices of a brie-type cheese deep fried in batter, with rice and vegetables, followed by a jelly full of tinned fruit. We retired to our sleeping bags well satisfied, and I for one slept like the proverbial top.

We awoke to another misty, moisty morning, the porters moving like phantoms as they dismantled the camp and loaded up. The onward track from Lasha skirted south of Phalung and then descended slowly to the floor of the Lasha Chu valley near the end of the area of the meanders. On the scree slopes beside the track we found a new plant, *Eriophyton wallichii*, a neat pyramid of overlapping leaves and bracts all densely covered in white hairs. The flowers, which resemble those of bugle, lay hidden under the woolly flaps, protected from the rain and snow. The plant had a fanciful resemblance to the woolly trolls one finds in toy shops.

Birdwatching was almost impossible in the driving rain, which had successfully grounded anything foolish enough to endeavour to fly, although a single young lammergeier and an adult golden eagle flew low over our heads before disappearing into the murk.

We followed the west bank of the Lasha Chu for some hours over fairly level ground, which gave us the opportunity to examine the plants growing alongside the river. We found more of the dramatic *Saxifraga cordigera*, a delicate flowered *Cremanthodium thomsonii* and clumps of

Swertia multicaulis – a relative of the gentians, with many short spikes of dark blue flowers surrounded by narrow, floppy leaves.

Eriophyton wallichii

We had hoped to cross the river and camp near the foot of the Sebu La, but the foul weather and our slow progress caused the porters to insist on pitching camp in good time, where the altitude was lower and the site warmer. This proved wise, as the next camp was high up, cold and exposed. We made a short excursion further up the valley which turned north as it narrowed, and gave tantalising glimpses of a deep cwm surrounded by cliffs and snow peaks. Heavy rain drove us all under cover, where the thrice blessed cook smilingly produced plates of deep fried brie balls and mugs of hot tea.

In the darkness of the night I could hear the river raging a few yards away, with the deep rumble of boulders being rolled along in the torrent, not a reassuring noise as we should have to wade the river next morning.

The crossing was a miserable business, as we waded barefoot through deep, ice cold water, and the loaded porters had a difficult time in the strong current to avoid being swept off their feet, despite a rope strung across the worst part of the crossing. There then followed a long, very steep haul up the mountainside to a hanging valley, which made us appreciate how wise the porters had been to insist on camping by the river. There was no proper track, just a jumble of boulders, but we forgot all the hard work in the excitement of the flowers we now found.

It was clear that few people or grazing animals ever crossed the river at this point, and this was reflected in the rich abundance of the flowers. The most striking feature was the wild rhubarb, *Rheum nobile*, many thousands of plants stretching up the steep black hillsides into the mists as far as the eye could see. Some superb specimens stood 2m high, and with their habit of growing in lines, presumably as the wind blew the seed, one could understand their being mistaken for the figures of soldiers. The blue poppies *Meconopsis horridula* and *M.simplicifolia* grew in similar abundance, although sadly battered by the weather. Among the rocks and on the edges of the little streams were bright sky-blue patches of *Corydalis ecristata* and several species of white and yellow saxifrages. White centred *Primula primulina* was plentiful, with the long leaves of *P.macrophylla* which was well past its flowering time, but best of all were the tiny gem-like flowers of *P.sapphirina*. This is a very small mauvey-blue primula, with nodding heads of single flowers and tiny, delicate, divided leaves almost fern-like in texture.

We climbed steadily upwards through a jumbled mass of rock, which I did find troublesome, since I could not use my left arm to support myself when I slipped, and on the wet rocks this was a frequent occurrence. I soon forgot my troubles when we came upon the extraordinary flowers of *Saussurea gossypiphora*. This was one of the flowers which I had wanted to see above all else. It has a wide Himalayan distribution on high altitude screes but, like the giant rhubarb, it had always eluded me. Imagine a soft, woolly rugby football set up on end, with sharp green leaves emerging from the wool, and you have a good idea of this weird plant. At first there seems to be no sign of a flower, but when the plant is mature the top of the football opens out to reveal a dome of purplish, tightly packed

Flowers by the banks of the Lasha Chu

Above left: Rheum nobile

Left: Corydalis ecristata

Right: Primula sapphirina

daisy flowers deep inside. This remarkable mechanism protects the vital flowers from the worst of the weather, a marvellous example of a plant adapting to a hostile environment.

We reached our camp site at noon, where it was perched on a spur at 5500m just below the Sebu La. Torrential rain was falling, with water running everywhere between the black rocks, while above in the mist we could occasionally see huge overhanging cliffs of ice. Massive scree slopes surrounded us and disappeared thousands of metres down into the valley. My tent chose this opportunity to spring a leak in the groundsheet, so a puddle steadily grew and everything got soaked. All evening I had a steady trickle of porters coming to my tent seeking treatment for headaches, upset stomachs and even, in the case of the cook's assistant, a badly burned wrist. A well stocked first-aid kit is absolutely essential for the well-being of any trekking group.

The weather pattern seemed fairly consistent. Mornings would be reasonable, overcast with just a hint of drizzle, but the afternoons and evenings were totally foul. Despite the miserable camp site, the cook cheered everyone up with an excellent dinner, although I did have a slight problem with the dish of tinned goat, which appeared to have suffered a severe accident before it was

Saussurea gossypiphora

West side of the Sebu La

Above: Primula concinna

Right: Corydalis meifolia

Porters on the Sebu La

canned: everything was full of needle sharp splinters of bone.

Our mountaineer, Lakhpa Tsering, had gone on ahead over the pass to check our route, and returned the same evening despite the awful weather – a remarkable effort. He had found the ice and snow conditions over the main Sebu La to be dangerous, and advised us to go south and then east, crossing by a pass of equal height some half a kilometre south of the main Sebu La.

Everyone had a miserable time packing up and striking the tents in pouring rain, but eventually it eased a little and we set off. The first section of the climb was a real slog over unstable screes and rock slides, slowly gaining altitude but very tiring. We reached one peak only to descend again, and plod up and down over a series of spurs descending from peaks on both the north and south of the route. Much of it was very

unstable, and everyone had to beware rocks dislodged by companions higher up. One porter slipped on the edge of a big drop, and was saved only by the quick action of those nearest him.

In such an inhospitable and unstable area, covered by snow and ice for much of the year, it was amazing to find any flowers, yet deep in among the shelter of the rocks were masses of tiny pink *Primula concinna*, *Corydalis meifolia* with feathery blue-green foliage and yellow flowers tipped with black, and many different saxifrages and androsaces. Each primula flower had a huge round drop of water caught in the throat of the flower, acting as a magnifying glass.

With the weather threatening to worsen, there was no desire to stay to botanise, and we pressed steadily on to the top of the Sebu La, which we reached at midday. The final section was extremely steep and slippery, and finished with huge stone slabs sloping upwards like the roof of a house. Our altimeters gave us a reading of 5900m – this was not a tourist route!

We took the obligatory photographs and spent a little while getting our breath back, before tackling the equally steep descent to the Sebu Tso. The first 300m consisted of scree alternating with patches of powdery snow all the way down to a tiny bright blue lake, but then the gradient eased off and it was pleasant going all the way to our camp site, which we reached two hours after leaving the top of the pass. There was an almost palpable sense of relief and lifting of tension as we relaxed in camp. Even the weather relented, giving us the finest, driest afternoon we had experienced since we left Thanggu. It was still a day's journey to Yume Samdong, but now it was all downhill, and a holiday atmosphere took over.

David, Usha and I, accompanied by the two botanically inclined porters, set out to walk round the nearest of the lakes, which Hooker had reached from the east in 1849. Despite a

Primula tenuiloba

Khangchengyao at dawn

Diapensia himalaica

Arenaria bryoides

rather bleak aspect, the flat valley floor around our camp proved rich in plants. Primulas grew in abundance, including *Primula tenuiloba*, pale mauve with elegant, long petals deeply cleft growing from dense cushions of tiny, bright green leaves. All the corydalis and saxifrages we had found as we climbed up to the Sebu La were plentiful here as well. We found another species of Saussurea, *S.hookeri*, with black tipped flowers like a slender knapweed, and several tiny annual gentians including *Gentiana infelix*. The bright blue flowers were all tightly closed for the lack of sunshine.

After dinner the porters invited us all into the big mess tent, where they entertained themselves and us with a lively song and dance session. Space limited the scope of the dances, but not of the songs. One man would start a song and then others would take over, improvising verses as they went along. From the shrieks of mirth of the onlookers, it was clear that many of the verses were highly personal in nature, and I have not the slightest doubt that we strange botanists featured in some of them. It was very good fun, and sent us all warm and happy to our sleeping bags. The skies cleared for the first time since we arrived in Sikkim, giving a night of moon and stars, so that we saw the whole vast Khangchengyao massif magically lit by moonlight.

At dawn the skies were still clear with just a few wisps of cloud filling the lower valleys. To the north of us the whole of Khangchengyao shone in the early light. The name translates as 'The bearded Kanchin', the beard being represented by the huge icefall which tumbles down the south face of the mountain. From where we camped, the peak of Khangchengyao was shaped like the roof of a vast house, while away to the east the peak of Gurudongmar showed as a white dome. Everywhere we looked were ranks of great snow peaks, but very soon the clouds rolled up again to obscure them. The second lake of Sebu Tso lay below us to the east, looking like a sheet of burnished steel in the dawn light, behind which were more great icefalls tumbling down from black peaks.

Immediately behind our tents David found a bank of *Diapensia himalaica*, tiny bronze leaves almost obscured by a sheet of bright pink, yellow-eyed flowers. Dwarf *Rhododendron nivale*, with crinkled mauve flowers, sprawled over the rocks, and on the screes nearby grew huge green pillows of *Arenaria bryoides*, studded with tiny white flowers.

While I was sitting in camp, I had time to study the country to the north, and it seemed at the time that there were three valleys draining down from the northern border which could prove of great interest botanically. All would be reachable from a base camp at Yume Samdong. The first ran from the icefall below Gurudongmar down to the level of the lowest of the lakes of the Sebu Tso. The second was the valley due north from Yume Samdong towards the Donkya La, a short distance below which it forked north-east to the foot of the Donkya Ri. An old map of 1903 noted limestone rock there, a discovery made by Joseph Hooker, with hot springs close by. Such a geological mix would almost certainly hold some interesting plants. The third valley, the Tembawa Chu valley, went due east from Yume Samdong. We spent the next day exploring it all too briefly, and found it sufficiently interesting to warrant spending much more time there.

I should dearly have liked to spend several days camped at the Sebu Tso, but time was pressing and we descended to Yume Samdong. After about a kilometre from the campsite we started the long descent down a grassy slope covered with flowers. The views south to Chombu and the glaciers flowing down from it were magnificent. Lakhpa Tsering had been in the recent party which had successfully climbed Chombu, and he rated it as 'difficult'. It looked awe-inspiring from where we were standing, a sharp white spire, with masses of tumbled ice descending from it in wave upon wave. I should not have

wanted the responsibility of picking a suitable route for an ascent.

There was no track for us to follow, although we could easily pick out the valley winding away to the east between great black cliffs. Above them perched glaciers which seemed ready to crash down at any moment, held up by nothing more than friction, while whole sections of mountain had recently broken away leaving raw scars of paler rock and mud.

Just for once the sun shone out of a blue sky, so we could descend the grassy slope at a leisurely pace and enjoy the flowers we found. Many of them were now old friends, with *Lilium nanum* here in its mauve-flowered form, the robust yellow lampshade

Chombu

flowers of *Cremanthodium nepalense* and the curious club-shaped inflorescences of *Soroseris hookerana*, the soft dun coloured 'stem' crowned with a flat disc of yellow flowers. Among the rocks at the foot of the slope was the biggest clump of *Meconopsis horridula* I had ever seen, all the flowers in pristine condition, the sky blue petals and golden anthers glowing in the sunshine. I could perhaps be forgiven for getting down on my knees before such a vision of loveliness, but it was also the best position from which to take a photograph.

We had now to pick our way along extensive ridges, rockfalls and grassy mounds, crossing innumerable streams to the edge of a large lake. The recent bad weather had washed away a rocky causeway, through which the deep river now roared in spate. There was no chance of a crossing, so we had to detour all the way round the lake, crossing all the feeder streams which were also in flood. Once past that obstruction we came upon a really good track down to Yume Samdong, past the famous hot springs. The local people had built a fine new stone bath hut, roofed with wooden shingles, into which the water was piped, somewhat sulphurous but at a gorgeous hot bath temperature which was wonderfully soothing to the travel worn. Some of the braver souls went for total immersion, while others, myself included, were content just to dangle our legs in the water, possibly mindful of the dictum 'You don't know where it's been'.

The mists now closed in on us as we strolled through the rather overgrazed yak pastures, but even here there were some fine plants. We had seen plenty of *Primula capitata* in many places at lower altitude, but here it

East to Yume Samdong

Camp-site at Yume Samdong

grew in profusion and as fine as I had ever seen it, great fat round heads of deep purple flowers on top of blue-green stems, and leaves covered in fine silvery farina. With them grew *Silene gonosperma*, another gem of a flower, each shaped like a round lampshade, the calyx ribs outlined in fine reddish hairs like velvet. We reached the road at last and turned uphill to our camp. Everyone was very tired, and for once I needed an aspirin for a headache. The cook provided another excellent supper, but most of us had small appetites.

Although yesterday the porters had sworn never to cross the Sebu La again, they were now aiming to cross back over to Lasha in a single day, albeit without loads. The Gut and his merry men had gone on ahead down to Lachung, having probably decided that we posed no further threat to security. Very early next morning our porters departed in high spirits, the two youngest running up the track like mountain goats. The mountain gods had at last relented, giving us a glorious sunny morning, which we had every intention to enjoy to the full. When Hooker had been in Yume Samdong he had travelled up the Tembawa Chu valley, which runs almost due east. To my knowledge no westerner had been there since, which gave an added attraction to our excursion.

David, Usha, Dr Sinha and I set off north for a short distance, past a summer shieling where a lone herdsman was milking his yaks. I tried to take some photographs, but the yaks would not tolerate a stranger near them. Rather than add to the herdsman's exasperation, I had to content myself with taking some telephoto shots from a respectable distance.

We crossed a new bridge spanning the river coming down from the Donkya La and began a long, slow ascent of 500m up a ridge covered in flowers. From the top of the ridge the track then turned east and descended to the valley floor, where it followed the course of the Tembawa Chu. The valley was really lovely, with meadows of flowers below the steep slopes soaring up to snow covered ridges. Here was evidence of the 1994 landslip disaster, with the now empty lake bed covered in bleached rocks. The escaping water had torn a huge channel 15m across and 10m deep, at the bottom of which a small trickle of water still flowed, fed by the snow fields higher up the valley.

There I left the others intent on collecting plant specimens, and walked on alone through the yak pastures, each twist of the valley bringing fresh views of the peaks and icefalls at its head. The whole scene was made magical by the utter silence. I heard a rattle of falling stones, and over a kilometre away on the opposite side of the valley I could just pick out a small flock of bharal grazing on the cliff ledges. Among the carpet of flowers were masses of blue *Cyananthus incanus*, with a yellow flowered species that was probably *C.spathulifolius*, and what appeared to be the hybrid between them. This had petals striped with blue and yellow, the throat of each flower filled by a big tuft of

Primula capitata

Cyananthus aff.spathulifolius

Meconopsis horridula

white hairs. I walked on over a series of moraine ridges to where I could see right up into the head of the valley, ringed by black cliffs topped by huge wind-sculpted cornices of snow and ice. Across the vertical black rock face ran wide horizontal bands of paler, blue-grey rock. Clouds and mist were starting to spill over the mountain tops from the east, so I returned to my companions as the rain descended once more.

Our return was hampered by thick mist, such that David and I missed our outward bound track entirely and fetched upon the edge of the Tembawa Chu where it runs through a ravine. A brief break in the mist enabled us to get our bearings on the camp and return safely.

Next morning was fine, but with a strong wind which kept the temperature down. Hooker complained of the windiness of Yume Samdong! Our transport back to Gangtok was due after breakfast, but the hours went by and nothing appeared. Finally at midday we heard the sound of vehicles coming up the valley, and hastened down to camp. Ganden and his team had been given an extraordinary message by Gut Lepcha, to the effect that all the porters and camp staff had left David, Henry and me on our own at Yume Samdong. Seriously concerned, he had wasted hours trying to confirm the story and find out what really had happened. The Gut was very odd.

The valley between Yume Samdong and Yumthang was most spectacular, with the road running on the west side of the valley which was bounded by huge cliffs. Every few kilometres there would be a gap in this wall of rock, with snow fields sweeping up to the high peaks behind. The whole area appeared uninhabited, and there was no sign of the heavy over-grazing which had been such a notable feature of the valley in which we had been travelling.

The new bridge at Tung was completed, so we sped on as far as the Meyong Chu,

which we reached in the late afternoon. There we were halted, since no progress had been made in spanning the gap where the road and bridge had been swept away. Once again we had to unload all our gear and portage it across the slide, the crossing proving muddier and more slippery than on the outgoing journey. Constant human traffic had led to further collapse of the temporary track, and we ended up sliding down, clinging to muddy tree roots to avoid falling off. Passing us in the opposite direction was a group of little schoolgirls, immaculate in blue and white uniforms, white socks and polished shoes. I looked at my own mud-spattered gear, and wondered how on earth they managed it. Tashi Lachungpa crossed ahead of us and returned triumphantly some time later with a jeep he had commandeered at the next village. We reached Gangtok well after dark, for a much needed bath and a welcome beer.

The next few days were spent in meetings with government departments, dividing up the collection of pressed specimens to be left behind, and enjoying some spectacularly good meals with our friends. There was an element both of surprise and delight that we had managed to complete our journey as planned, despite the weather.

On our final evening Tashi and Wangyal presented me with a magnificent thanka depicting the goddess Dolma. The 'Green Dolma' of the Tibetans is a very popular deity, besought as the 'unloosener of difficulties'. She appears in the form of a bejewelled young Indian woman of green complexion, seated on a lotus and holding a

Dolma – Goddess of Compassion

long-stemmed lotus flower. She now hangs in pride of place in my home, a constant reminder of my good friends in Sikkim. This gift to me, a veterinary surgeon, was particularly apt, since two of the prayers offered to Dolma are as follows: 'That the burdens of all animals will be lightened' and 'We beseech thee, by whatever merit we have accumulated, to kindly regard all the animals'.

I was left with the hope that there might be a little merit left over to permit me one day to return to the mountains of Sikkim, and particularly to the valleys above Yume Samdong.

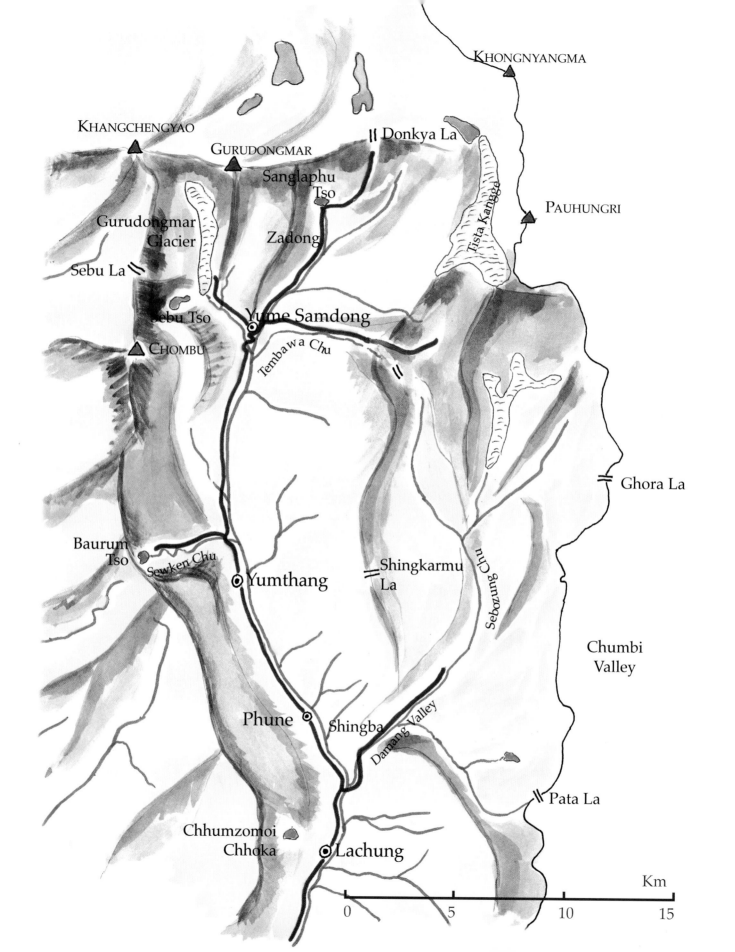

2001 A Sikkim Odyssey

Leycesteria formosa
Gurudongmar

*F*ive years were to pass before I was able once more to travel to Sikkim. Not that I had deserted the mountains – far from it . . .

In 1998 I trekked in east Nepal, walking from Suketar first to the south side of Khangchendzonga above Oktang, and then over the Mirgin La and Sinion La passes to Ghunsa and the north side of Khangchendzonga beyond Kambachen.

The following year I was in Tibet, first at Lhasa and then in the south-east at Showa, close to where the Tsang-po loops down through the Himalaya to emerge as the Brahmaputra in India. After crossing and returning over the Showa La, I travelled north with my companions to Bago, from where we walked over the Nambu La to Pasum Tso, before returning to Lhasa.

During this time I had been discussing the possibility of returning to Sikkim, and in particular to the valleys north of Yume Samdong, towards the border with Tibet – valleys which had fired my curiosity as we descended from the Sebu La in 1996. Since my previous travels in Sikkim had been in spring and summer, it seemed a good idea to make my fourth trip in the autumn, to photograph the autumn flowers and the gentians in particular.

Access to north Sikkim is never easy, requiring special permission from the Indian military authorities in Delhi, over and above the visas and restricted area permits which all foreigners need in order to travel in the state. The correspondence file grew alarmingly, but, despite comforting noises which issued at irregular intervals from the authorities, nothing actually happened. Experienced travellers will have met this procedure the world over, but the very nature of the Indian bureaucratic machine renders it even more mind-bogglingly tortuous.

Travel of the type that I was planning is never cheap, and one is loth to spend large sums of money for a journey which may never take place. By the middle of August 2000 I was no further forward, so with great regret I abandoned any hope of reaching Sikkim in that year.

Instead I joined a delightful group of like-minded individuals on a walk from Paro in west Bhutan, along the Himalayan chain through Laya and Lunana to Jakar in

Rainbow over the Tista

the east, most of the time under clear blue skies and bright sunshine.

While we relaxed at Jakar at the end of the trip, there occurred one of those bizarre episodes which stress the remarkable manner in which the East has embraced electronic technology, while other aspects of life there remain positively medieval. Around us were gorgeous ancient palaces and temples, while one villager had a computer, solar powered, and was obviously on the Internet.

'Where do you come from?' was the inevitable question, to which I replied 'From Lewes in Sussex, a place in the south of England.'

'Oh, my God! Your town is under water!'

This was November 2000, when so much of Britain had suffered disastrous flooding, but to learn of it in eastern Bhutan was a little unnerving.

Back home, I returned to the fray, writing and telephoning with a frequency which must have appalled the unfailingly courteous staff at the Indian High Commission in London. It reached a stage where I did not need to give my name. They knew – dear God, they knew!

The Tista valley

In Sikkim I placed the logistical planning in the very capable hands of Ganden Lachungpa in Gangtok, while my good friend Mohan Pradhan indicated his desire to accompany me and agreed to supervise the overall planning in Sikkim. Both were to prove vital to the whole project, but there must have been times when they wondered just what they had taken on.

By early July planning was in an advanced stage, with detailed itineraries and tickets purchased for both international and internal flights. I was repeatedly told that a restricted area permit was all that I needed – no problem! – while I knew perfectly well from experience in 1996 that this was not so, and that an additional protected area permit would be demanded. It later transpired that this could only be issued by the military authorities in Delhi, and that I should have to travel out as

arranged and just hope that it could be obtained once I was there. So it was with grave forebodings that I duly arrived in Gangtok at the end of August, and found that matters were exactly as I had feared.

The next four days were highly stressful, with hopes seeming about to be fulfilled, only to be dashed. Telephone calls, faxes and e-mails flew in all directions, while my good friends in Gangtok did everything in their power to help. I was singularly blessed with their assistance, acting as they were from positions of considerable authority. Without their help I should have had to return to Britain without ever having reached my goal.

My mood was mirrored by the weather, with everything blanketed in cloud so thick that I could barely see beyond the street opposite, while rain fell in torrents and the roads ran like rivers.

In the midst of all the furore I took a very necessary break to go down into Gangtok, where I found the town *en fête*, for this was the celebration of Pang-Lhab-sol, an annual commemoration of a pact of brotherhood made in the 13th century between the Lepcha people and the Bhotias.

History relates how Khye Bhumsa, a Bhotia prince of Kham Minyak in Tibet, settled at Phari in the Chumbi valley. Sadly his marriage to Jomo Guru was childless, and he therefore sought the advice of the religious authorities. They prophesied that a Lepcha seer in the land in the south would be able to grant him the boon of children, so he set off with his retinue, reaching the site of present-day Lingchom. There he met an elderly Lepcha couple busy working in their fields, and enquired of them where the Lepcha seer could be found.

Gangtok from the helicopter

Thekong Tek, with his wife Nyo-kung-Ngal, entertained Khye Bhumsa, revealing that he was indeed the seer for whom they were searching, and after listening to his request he gave the prince his blessing. Khye Bhumsa then returned home, where a year later his wife bore him a son. In gratitude for this miracle, Khye Bhumsa returned in the following year, when a treaty of blood brotherhood between the Bhotias and Lepchas was sealed. This has been celebrated annually until the present day, and in 1996 a fine statue depicting the historic meeting was consecrated.

Around this statue a large marquee had been erected, with an elaborate altar decorated with butter lamps and bowls of offerings. Monastic leaders and local dignitaries were all assembling for the speeches and celebrations, the lamas in red robes and mitres. Naturally curious, I had stopped to take a photograph, but was promptly grabbed and warmly invited to come in and take part. Conscious of my none-too-smart appearance I tried to demur, but my new friends were having none of it, and I duly found myself seated with the 'nobs' for a very enjoyable and colourful ceremony.

Afterwards processions of decorated floats and school children in colourful costumes paraded along the Mahatma Gandhi Marg, followed by teams of folk dancers and dancers in fabulous masks. The children, although obviously there under orders (how many of us have suffered similarly in our youth!), were in high spirits, singing lustily – although from the expressions on the faces of some of the accompanying teachers, the version being sung was probably not the official one!

The Abbot of Rumtek Monastery at Gangtok, celebrating Pang-Lhab-Sol

Decorated floats outside the Sikkim Tourism offices

School children parading along the Mahatma Gandhi Marg at Pang-Lhab-Sol

Goodyera repens

Begonia picta

Returning to the hotel I found no messages waiting, nor any sign of the hoped-for permits. At this stage our plan was to drive north from Gangtok first to Lachung, and then up to Yume Samdong. There we would establish our base camp, with a view to exploring and camping in the three valleys, north-west to Gurudongmar, north towards the Donkya La and east up the Tembawa Chu valley. Ganden was busy making all the arrangements for transport, porters and camping, but I had some time on my hands and visited the Gangtok Zoo Park, set on the ridge above the town in a well wooded area.

I am no lover of zoos as such, but I can recommend an afternoon there if only to see the wild flowers and birds which flourish within the boundaries. As it was now early September, most of the small migrant passerines had left, but I had excellent views of white-throated fantail flycatcher, white-browed and golden bush robins, red-billed leiothrix, brown flycatcher, whiskered yuhina (its crest always reminding me of a punk hairstyle), a flock of white-winged grosbeaks and dark blue whistling thrushes wherever a stream flowed down the hills.

The wild flowers were equally enjoyable, big bushes of blue *Hydrangea macrophylla*, scarlet-fruited *Leycesteria formosa*, tall, golden spires of the ginger relative *Hedychium spicatum*, little pink *Begonia picta* on the moss covered rocks, blue *Swertia multicaulis*, spikes of the little pink orchid *Anthiogonium gracile* in profusion, and in the moss under pine trees the small, white-flowered orchid *Goodyera repens*. The latter I knew well, growing in Speyside in Scotland in just the same sort of habitat.

The following day I took an incredibly bumpy taxi ride to Rangka on the valley slopes west of Gangtok, which had been recommended as 'good for flowers'. Although I followed a series of tracks along the hillside, cultivation was intensive and few wild flowers remained, but the trip did give me the opportunity to visit Zurmang monastery, a striking new complex where building began in 1992, and is still in progress. The whole design was spacious, beautifully set out and decorated in exquisite traditional style. The main prayer hall was magnificent, richly decorated in red and gold.

Zurmang monastery

I returned to the hotel to find Ganden and Mohan waiting for me and looking decidedly glum. Shortly before I arrived in Sikkim two Russians had been arrested for illegally collecting thousands of butterflies and moths. It appeared that they had entered Sikkim from Nepal without permits and had been active for some time before the police caught up with them. It was also rumoured that they were well known for such activities and that the authorities in Russia were in no hurry to have them back.

Understandably the Indian Government was in no mood to sanction another foreigner in north Sikkim, and it seemed highly unlikely that I should ever get the permits I so desperately needed. I must admit that it was deeply depressing that I should get so close to success after so many years, only to be stymied through no fault of my own. As a last resort I sent a fax message to the Indian High Commission in London, who had viewed my plans favourably, in the folorn hope that they might persuade the military authorities in Delhi. To our utter astonishment we received a return fax with all the necessary documentation. We were free to go north, with permission to visit all the areas I had hoped to see, with the result that a day which had opened in the depths of gloom finished in elation.

The following day I had a long and profitable discussion with Dr A.S. Chauhan, the joint director of the Botanical Survey of India, Himalayan Circle, who supervise all botanical recording in the state. The authorities required me to sign a declaration that I would not collect any plant material whatsoever, although I was free to take photographs. It was also required that a scientist should supervise my activities, to

The main prayer hall at Zurmang monastery

ensure that there could be no repetition of the Russian scandal. I was fortunate to be accompanied by Dr Paramjit Singh, who proved to be not only a highly skilled botanist but a most congenial companion.

The next thirty-six hours were spent running round in circles, taking copies of permits, visas and innumerable documents to various government departments. The photocopy of my police permit turned out very oddly. My sunburned complexion and white hair caused great amusement, as it made me 'look like a plainsman'!

It was wonderful to relax in that glow of pleasurable anticipation which is the prelude to a trip such as the one we had planned, when everything seems possible. At a dinner party with my friends that evening I heard how, in the villages of Lachung and Lachen, local affairs are

Arundina graminifolia

Dendrobium hookerianum

Ama Tshering Bhutia, owner of the teahouse at Bakcha Chu

decided by a village council on which each household is represented, under the headship of an elected 'pipon'. State law does not apply. Decisions are made as to the dates on which grazing stock shall move up or down to pasture according to the seasons, and if an official visitor is to be entertained in the village it is decided which households shall provide shelter, food or fuel. I was also told the story of one of Joseph Hooker's porters, who was sent back to Yume Samdong to find an irreplaceable barometer which had been mislaid. A sudden heavy snow storm and bitter cold made Hooker fear for the man's safety, but the resourceful porter spent all night immersed in the hot springs there and returned next day in good spirits, bearing the precious instrument.

On September 6 we finally set off in thick mist after heavy overnight rain, which made us anxious that parts of the road ahead might have washed away. I also wondered whether the elderly lady who owned the teahouse at the Bakcha Chu would still be active, and it was with considerable delight that I found Ama Tshering as sprightly as ever, seemingly unchanged by the passing years. Nearby a number of spikes of *Arundina graminifolia*, the bamboo orchid, were in full flower, their big mauve blooms seeming to glow on the steep rocks beside the road. More exciting was the sight of *Dendrobium hookerianum*, a rare, golden yellow orchid with large flowers. These bear two rich brown spots like eyes, and a deeply fringed lip, unlike its more common relative *D.chrysanthum*, which grows in the trees all around Gangtok.

To my relief the road at Tung, which had proved such a problem in 1996, was in good shape and we passed without trouble. A brief pause near the river produced plumbeous redstart, white-cheeked bulbul and Tibetan shrike, while overhead three black eagles circled slowly, high in the sky.

We reached our destination at Lachung by mid-afternoon, staying in a simple but extremely comfortable lodge. This lay at the foot of an impressive waterfall, which dropped nearly 2500ft in a series of cascades from the cliffs above the village. Lachung is a large village which straggles along the road and across the river to a fine gompa set on the hill among pine trees. The style of the houses is attractive, most of them being single storey wooden structures set up on stilts or stone pillars, with wood for fuel stacked underneath. The older houses had nicely carved doorposts and window frames, but most had been modernised to some extent, with corrugated iron roofs replacing the original wooden shingles. Newly-built houses continued in the traditional style.

I was particularly keen to see if any dating from Hooker's time in the mid-19th century still existed. On questioning some of the older inhabitants I was directed to two little houses nestling among the trees right beside the gompa. They had never

Traditional house by the gompa at Lachung

Lachung

been 'improved', and looked exactly like those which Hooker had sketched. It seems that they were the only such houses that remained. Each was quite small, raised on substantial stone built pillars, with a wide, chalet-style roof covered in wooden shingles, and walls constructed of wooden panels on a timber frame. Both the door frames and windows were edged with simple carving. Under the house the space was, as customary, stacked with wood as fuel for the winter. I was not able to see inside, as my companions explained quietly that the lama who lived there was at prayer.

Less pleasing was the new hotel, four storeys high and bright pink in colour, that had been erected at the west end of Lachung. Certainly it offers comfortable accommodation to tourists, but such an ugly excrescence was totally out of keeping with the charming style of Lachung houses.

Once more the rain fell in torrents, but we were comfortable, warm and dry, while our cook Gyapo Bhutia produced an excellent supper. I was delighted to find orchid photographs that I had taken at Thanggu in

Mother and baby, Lachung

Neottianthe secundiflora

orchid. It may be common, but it is gorgeous to look at! Overhead, yellow-billed choughs and Himalayan swiftlets were circling like gnats, high in the sky among the clouds, while around me in the trees rufous turtle-doves called and large flocks of long-tailed minivets twittered, the males resplendent in scarlet and cobalt blue.

Since we were spending the day in Lachung, partly to arrange for porters but also to acclimatise to the higher altitude of 3000m, I took the opportunity to explore the slopes above the village. As we climbed a narrow zigzag road uphill, we passed the house of the Lachung Rimpoche, who is a re-incarnation in the same manner as the Dalai Lama. The boys suggested we should call on him, although I was not so sure that he would want to see me. However, he proved most courteous and kindly, and we were invited into his prayer room. The room was simple but bright, with a highly polished parquet floor of contrasting wooden tiles. The Rimpoche sat on a raised cushion behind a small decorated table, on which were placed his ceremonial objects which included a gorgeous whisk of peacock feathers. His servant gave us tea while he conversed through my companions, since my own command of the language was sadly inadequate.

He was very interested to know that I had been in Bhutan, and especially that I had also been to Lhasa and to eastern Tibet. I was closely questioned on what I had seen there, the state of the monasteries and the degree of religious freedom permitted by the Chinese nowadays after the destruction wrought during the Cultural Revolution. We were then blessed and presented with knotted red silk cords to hang around our

1989 reproduced on large posters on the walls of the lodge as part of the promotion of tourism in Sikkim.

Early next morning I walked out of the village to the north, following the road as it twisted and climbed towards Yakchey. Even within the village boundary the roadside wild flowers were interesting, especially where steep rocky banks could not be reached by the grazing cows and goats which wandered at will. Three little orchids grew in profusion, pink-flowered *Satyrium nepalense* and *Neottianthe secundiflora*, and the tight, spiral flower spikes of *Spiranthes sinensis*, each tiny floret intensely dark pink with a contrasting white lip. *Euphorbia sikkimensis* was beginning to develop an orange flush at the approach of autumn, while *Rhododendron lepidotum* sported some yellow blooms out of season. On the road verge *Roscoea purpurea* grew in plenty, each short stem crowned with a massive purple flower which much resembled a large necks, while in addition he placed a kata (ceremonial silk scarf) over my shoulders. At the time the boys treated the affair lightly, but as time went by and our luck repeatedly turned out so well , they began to have second thoughts on the efficacy of the Rimpoche's blessing. I shall remember his warm smile.

From his house the climb was steep, and I was soon puffing and blowing as I had yet to get fully acclimatised. Everywhere we found the same little orchids I had found earlier around the village, and drifts of the purple *Roscoea*. As we stopped to shelter from a particularly heavy burst of rain I spotted a bright yellow flower on a steep rock face. On climbing up, I found several plants of the delightful orchid *Spathoglottis*

ixioides, which I had previously seen at Lachen in 1996.

By now the wind and rain were beating down, so we retreated, only to realise that were covered in hundreds of leeches. We spent the next quarter of an hour picking them off ourselves and each other, never an easy job as they loop round so quickly and restick themselves on to your fingers.

Later that evening we sat round the warm stove in the lodge, while Ganden told the locals about the trip we had done together over the Sebu La in north Sikkim, and other journeys I had made. They were horrified at what I was now planning to do, and so was I when I discovered that two little old men sitting in the corner were ten and fifteen years younger than I was!

Roscoea purpurea

Spathoglottis ixioides

The Lachung Rimpoche

Lachung gompa

159

Next day we loaded up in a lorry and a jeep for the four hour drive up to Yume Samdong, while the clouds lowered and the rain descended in torrents. We stopped for a break at Phune, where we had stayed briefly in 1996, but things had sadly changed in the intervening years. The nice old rest-house had been destroyed by fire, some say as the result of arson, the replacement being smaller and rather shabby. The surrounding forest reserve had been decimated by illegal logging. Where we had been unable to see the Lachung river through the trees was now an open space, with tree stumps and scattered rhododendron bushes. Later we were to see tree trunks being loaded on to lorries in broad daylight, and to witness this in a forest reserve was deeply disturbing.

We stopped again just north of the dak bungalow at Yumthang and briefly botanised in the forest alongside the road. *Goodyera repens* grew in abundance in the sheets of moss under the pine trees, which also sheltered the big red fruiting heads of *Arisaema griffithii* and delicate fronds of *Polygonatum verticillatum* bearing little pendant clusters of red berries.

Once again this stretch of forest was full of birds: white-capped redstarts, greenish warblers, grey crested tits and red-headed bullfinches all every bit as numerous as I remembered from my last visit.

The road north to Yume Samdong now climbed up, curve after curve, as it rose from 4,000m to more than 4,500m, all the time following the foaming Lachung Chu pouring down off the watershed with Tibet. On a very remote stretch of this tortuous road I was delighted to find a solitary traffic sign with the legend 'Bends'. Beside the road the vegetation became more and more alpine in character, and we left the last trees behind just north of the Sewken Chu. Even from the cab of the bouncing jeep I could identify various saxifrages, *Cassiope fastigiata*, *Potentilla arbuscula* with large golden yellow flowers making it the most attractive of its genus, and masses of a large blue *Cyananthus* which was to prove such a feature of the alpine slopes higher up the valley.

We stopped briefly to perform a puja for the success of our expedition and to erect a prayer flag, reaching Yume Samdong in mist so thick that I failed to recognise the place. The weather then started to clear, so with Siwa, one of our staff, and local guide Sonam I walked up to the hot springs beside the Sebu Chu.

The valley was every bit as good as I had remembered, with masses of sky blue *Gentiana ornata*, tiny dark blue *Aconitum hookeri*, three different louseworts (*Pedicularis oederi*, dwarf pink *P.siphonantha*

Damaged forest, Shingba. See page 125 for the same view taken five years earlier

and yellow *P.longiflora)*, *Gaultheria trichophylla* with its bright blue berries studding the turf everywhere, *Cassiope fastigiata* and *C.selaginoides* both in seed, *Silene gonosperma* with flowers like little striped lampshades, and finally on the river gravels a mass of the big, stalkless daisy heads of *Waldheimia glabra*, the pink petals seeming to glow above a dense mat of finely divided foliage. Dwarf rhododendrons of three different species carpeted the slopes, but as it was now autumn none of them was in flower.

Early morning started clear, with a large flock of bright blue grandala, the size of mistle thrushes, foraging on the edge of the camp while a flock of white winged snow pigeons circled overhead with a single

raven. At this stage I was anxious to explore the possibility of camping in the valley that runs north-west to the foot of Gurudongmar, since it looked most inviting on the map. We set off back to the hot springs and then struck north up the valley slopes to a long ridge which disappeared round the shoulder of a small peak. This proved surprisingly hard going, as there was no track, but I was amply rewarded by the richness of the flora, since the south facing slope received plenty of sun.

It was almost impossible to walk without treading on the flowers of *Gentiana ornata*, and here I found the two *Cyananthus* species we had seen on our drive up to Yume Samdong. *C.incanus* I knew well, but the other plant refused my attempts to identify

Aconitum hookeri

Gaultheria trichophylla

Waldheimia glabra

Khangchengyao west ridge from the hot springs

Gentiana ornata

Cyananthus aff. lobatus

Rheum nobile

Glacial valley below Gurudongmar

it. True, the large blue flowers resembled *C.lobatus*, but where that has the throat of the flower stuffed with white hairs, this plant had a wide open bare throat.

Two yellow saxifrages *S.aristulata* and *S.brachypoda* were also abundant, with clumps of deep pink *Arenaria melandryoides* and the tiny blue stars of *Gentiana micans* dotting the ground. In crevices in the rocks I found the sky blue *Corydalis ecristata* and the fat mauve flowers of the dwarf *Delphinium brunonianum*. As we climbed higher we came across more and more giant rhubarb *Rheum nobile*, some five foot tall spires still immaculately clad in bracts like cream-coloured handkerchiefs. We also found a few rather tattered and storm blown *Meconopsis horridula*, their glorious pale blue flowers somewhat shredded.

We had now reached the cliffs and screes at about 5,500m, which held more treasures: *Gentana urnula* with its tight clumps of almost geometrically arranged leaves, and tucked under the large rocks the miniscule *Primula sapphirina* with tiny bluish mauve flowers nestling above foliage almost like moss, the leaves were so small.

The ridge petered out as we turned the corner and found ourselves with a cliff soaring up on our right hand and a 200m drop to a glacial trough on our left, where the glacier below Gurudongmar had retreated. This invited serious climbing for which we were not prepared, and the glacial trough stretched for several miles up into the low cloud where the peak of the mountain was hiding. It was no place to make a camp, as it looked like an abandoned building site of jumbled rocks and grey mud, with precious little chance of finding any plants of interest growing there. So much for the attractive valley on the map!

We made our way back to the hot springs, where we found others of our party had come for a bath and were now enjoying the hospitality of two elderly ladies who were living there for the summer while they pastured their yaks. We were invited in for butter tea, which was most welcome, since we were tired and wet through. They were obviously intrigued by this odd European who had appeared, but as the conversation was in the Lachung dialect I could not follow it. However, by the hilarity which accompanied it and their looks at me I could guess much of it, especially as it finished with an invitation to stay the night! What did interest me was their report of a flock of some twenty takin (*Budorcas taxicolor*), a calf sized animal halfway in appearance between a sheep and a goat, which had been around their camp that morning. I never did see any sign of them during our stay at Yume Samdong, but others of our staff later spotted them about a mile away.

Next day dawned with thick mist and torrential rain, which delayed our start but

Family at the hot springs, with Siwa and Kumar

did give us the opportunity to discuss and rethink our plans. While we had been up the Sebu Chu, Ganden had walked north up to Zadong to make a reconnaissance for a camp site there. His report was not encouraging, as he found the area bleak and the ground saturated. There was only one place remotely suitable for camping, and that lay in the valley of the Sangla PhuTso to the west of the Donkya La.

The weather eased again, so we decided to attempt to reach the Sebu Tso lakes which

Alpine accentor

The view west to Sebu Tso

163

we had passed on our descent from the Sebu La, after crossing from Thanggu in 1996. To our dismay we found that an immense landslide had carried away the entire hillside down which we had come, one lake had vanished and another completely new one had formed. It also proved impossible to cross the Sebu Chu at the valley head without constructing a bridge. It would appear that our old route was destroyed, and in the time at our disposal it was not possible to discern a new way in which to reach the lakes and the pass above them.

While we had been disappointed, Dr Singh had made a nice discovery of the orchid *Goodyera fusca* just below camp, so in appalling light and dense mist Siwa, Gyapo and I walked down and confirmed his find. What was intriguing was the altitude at which it was growing – 5,100m, a good 500m higher than it had previously been recorded. It is a charming little orchid, rather like *Goodyera repens*, but with a fatter

Tembawa Chu valley

spike of larger cream coloured flowers which are sweetly scented and attract dozens of tiny midges.

We awoke after a bitterly cold night, to find snow had fallen 350m above us, while we had endured heavy rain which drummed on the tents and kept us awake. It requires a degree of self-control to wash and shave outside under these conditions, a problem made worse in my case by being desperately short-sighted. Spectacles become useless in the wet, and if you put them down you cannot find them again.

I very much wanted to revisit the Tembawa Chu valley east of our camp, so we took a chance on a slight improvement in the weather, crossing the river and climbing up the ridge which gives access to the valley. This is always a tiring slog, but the valley repays you amply for the effort. We skirted the site of the lake which had emptied so disasterously in 1994, and began recording the flowers in the first grazing meadow we reached.

The valley is traditionally divided into three grazing areas, 'Lhanga' near the old lake bed, 'Zshimu' the middle area and 'Lakhaghom', the far upper grazing. Lhanga was smothered in the big blue *Cyananthus* we had found at Yume Samdong, but here it grew with *Aconitum hookeri* in sufficient quantity to impart a blue haze to the pasture. Among the rocks I found more *Primula sapphirina*, and near the lower of the two yak herders huts Siwa spotted six bharal (blue sheep) accompanied by a single lamb. We pressed on to the middle part of the valley, but the weather closed in, with driving snow, and we retreated to camp.

Next morning the snow had fallen just above our camp and everything was veiled in thick mist. Our porters had a portable radio, and at breakfast time there was a sudden shout and everyone clustered round it. This was September 12, and we listened, appalled, to the news of the terrorist attacks on the World Trade Centre towers in New York on the previous day.

Almost immediately the radio stopped working, and it was not until a fortnight later, when we got back to Gangtok, that we heard the full story of what had happened. Without exception, we were all deeply affected by the news, and a pall of gloom descended on the camp, mirrored by the abysmal weather.

All of us were tired by our exertions on the previous day, but eventually Ganden, Sonam and I set out to explore the valley across the river to the south-east of our camp. On the way we stopped to talk to the local yak herders, and I took the opportunity to ask them whether the yaks suffered any ill effects from eating *Aconitum spicatum*,

Sonam milking a yak

Codonopsis foetans

Goodyera fusca

which I had always reckoned to be highly poisonous. I had observed that the yaks had stripped all the leaves but left the flowers at the top of the spikes alone. They replied that the yaks never eat the immature foliage in spring, only stripping the mature leaves in late summer. They agreed that the rhizomes were lethal, and I can only assume that the foliage is unpalatable and probably toxic early in the year, but that the poisonous alkaloid is absent from the old leaves. They also remarked that the yaks actively sought out the foliage of *Bistorta macrophylla*, which they seemed greatly to enjoy and upon which they thrive and fatten.

We walked down river to where the Tembawa Chu cuts through a gorge before joining the Sebu Chu. From the gorge we struck uphill through a tangle of dwarf rhododendron to reach a huge whale-back of bare granite 200m long, polished smooth by the action of glacial ice which had left an enormous erratic boulder perched on top, like the pea on the proverbial drum. The view should have been stunning, with the Sebu Chu and Zadong Chu flowing down to unite at the foot of the hill, but we could not see a thing in the thick cloud!

Despite the rain we found some good plants. This area seemed to be less heavily grazed and would merit a more extensive and detailed botanical survey. Giant rhubarb was plentiful, and I found a large colony of the orchid *Goodyera fusca* growing in moss among dwarf rhododendron bushes. We walked back through masses of *Codonopsis foetans*, an attractive looking flower like a big, drooping campanula, but aptly named as it stinks of fox urine. Back in camp we all retreated to our tents to get dry, even if we could not get warm.

Conditions were becoming increasingly difficult for everyone, as we had no capacity to dry anything and all our gear was becoming sodden. Dr Singh had obviously been incubating a cold before the trip, and his breathing was becoming increasingly stressed due to the infection coupled with effects of high altitude. Heavy snow began to fall, and we decided that he would go down in the vehicle which brought Mohan up to us, and that arrangements could then be made to evacuate camp the following day and move down to Yumthang where conditions would be easier.

While we waited for the jeep to arrive, the conversation turned to the subject of yeti. While admitting that some stories have become embellished over the years, I am firmly of the opinion that there remains a core of probability that they exist. The descriptions I had been given by herdsmen and villagers in west Sikkim and in Bhutan were consistent, and three types of yeti were described.

'Mingma' is the large yeti which features in most stories, and appears in paintings on temple walls, some of which clearly predate any European interest in the subject.

'Lam Lamay' is of middle size, some 1.25 –1.5m tall, covered in black hair and walking upright for much of the time. In many respects this would most closely resemble a large monkey.

'Megyoi' is small and hairy, about the size of a seven-year-old child. This type had been clearly described to me in 1987 by a Lepcha herdsman I met while we were camped at Dzongri in west Sikkim. Huge footprints are regularly seen in the snow in the upper Lachung valley, and for a short period in late November and early

December yeti are heard calling loudly in the upper regions of the forest. A large yeti was reportedly seen near Yumthang in 2000. Lack of evidence from western travellers is no proof that yeti do not exist. I have never seen a bear in ten trips in the eastern Himalaya, and yet they exist to the extent that they injure a substantial number of local people every year. When we visitors travel, we create too much noise and disturbance. Any self-respecting bear will promptly remove itself to the next valley, and one would expect the same to be true of a yeti, assuming also that it is possessed of greater intelligence than a bear.

While we were sitting talking, a rose-breasted pipit pottered into my tent and proceeded to walk right under my legs before making its way out again. Many of the mountain birds rarely encounter the human species, and since the population is almost entirely Buddhist they are never threatened. As a result they display a most endearing trust.

The Zadong Chu

Mohan Pradhan (left) and Dr Paramjit Singh at Yume Samdong

Below right: Saxifraga caveana

Halenia elliptica

Mohan duly arrived and Dr Singh left, by which time a substantial amount of snow had fallen. None of us wanted to sit around, so we set off north up the road towards the border with Tibet. The road followed the course of the Zadong Chu, which looked superb as it rushed over the rocks between banks of snow. Despite the poor visibility, we saw dozens of grandala, several family parties of rufous-breasted accentors and a single Eurasian dipper on the river bank. We walked on at a smart pace and suddenly realised that we had reached Zadong, where the road abruptly finishes. Beyond was a flat valley bottom, boggy and saturated, with a brief glimpse through the clouds of snow-covered slopes below the Donkya La. Ganden had been totally correct in deciding that it was an unpleasant place to camp.

At supper that night Ganden produced a bottle of a special Sikkimese whisky to cheer us up. I am not a whisky drinker, but we were all so chilled that it seemed an excellent idea. I have never in my life met anything to rival it. It not only bored a hole straight through the floor of my stomach, but continued downwards and drilled a hole in the soles of my boots. The mere thought of it still brings tears to the eyes, but in all fairness most Sikkimese whisky and brandy is thoroughly enjoyable. This brand was unique.

Next morning the lorry arrived and we loaded up the camp for the journey down to Yumthang. There we found the dak bungalow unoccupied, and once we had located the chowkidar we moved in. The bungalow was built on traditional colonial lines, with a pleasant wide verandah round three sides, which shelters one from the worst of the weather. The site is superb, overlooking the river, above which the forested slopes rise over 1000m to icefalls and glaciers. However it is dark and depressing, with tiny double-framed windows which scarcely admit any light. Even by day one had to grope around to locate the furniture, so candles and torches were essential. However, we were able to light fires, and soon had lines rigged to dry out our soaking wet clothing.

We took the opportunity to use the departing lorry to hitch a lift down some way below the Shingba forest and walked back to see what we could find. There the climate was palpably warmer, but this meant that many of the flowers were over or in seed, such as the tall spires of *Meconopsis paniculata*, the low growing alpines *Halenia elliptica*, *Gentiana elwesii* and an unidentifiable small green orchid which looked like a *Habenaria*. Many of the bushes were in fruit, *Gaultheria fragrantissima*, orange fruited *Rubus hypargyrus* and once again the bright blue berries of creeping *Gaultheria trichophylla* scattered all over the ground.

We came back along the river meadows, where I was delighted to hear the trilling calls of ibisbill. They had been breeding there when we saw them in 1996, but had failed to breed in the last three years.

Next morning dawned crystal clear, with a blue cloudless sky and stunning views north to distant snow peaks. Across the river from the bungalow the forest rose up over 700m, above which glaciers and icefalls gleamed in the sun. I made up my mind to try to reach them if any way could be found, but the locals were not sure that the old tracks still existed.

Some 2km north of Yumthang the Sewken Chu tumbles down from a high valley running north-west, and on the old maps a track was marked running up to lake called the Baurum Tso, and then right across to Lachen in the west. Again no one seemed sure what the route was like, but it promised to be interesting. We left the road

Yumthang on a fine morning

Aorchis spathulata

Yumthang from the Sewken Chu

by a bridge and struck up through splendid forest on an extremely steep path, which had us pausing frequently to recover our breath. The upper forest level was reached some 700m above the river valley at a place called Tsethang, where we could at last look back down to the Lachung Chu far below us. In the more open terrain we found white *Clematis montana*, tall blue *Swertia hookeri* and plenty of *Gentiana ornata*. Beside a stream grew the rather sinister looking chocolate coloured flowers of *Astragalus donianus* and yellow *Cremanthodium reniforme*, well named since the leaf resembles a cross-section of a kidney complete with deep set veins. Around us were dense stands of a pink berried bush, probably *Sorbus arachnoidea*.

Lunch was taken on top of a big rock called Bhamchek Lakha, and we then pushed on upwards with difficulty. The tangled mass of rhododendron was more than head high and virtually impenetrable

without a chopper, so what track there was tended to follow the top of more exposed ridges. These formed virtual islands of alpine flowers rising above a dense sea of rhododendron, and proved a rich hunting ground. The small purple orchid *Aorchis spathulata* grew in abundance with two species of *Habenaria*, but all of them were well past their flowering season. Two bright yellow saxifrages, *Saxifraga moorcroftiana* and *S.caveana* were tucked away in every available crevice, beside *Corydalis meifolia* with its attractive blue-green leaves, and the bizarre *Saussurea uniflora*, which had large inflated purple bracts below each single thistle-like flower.

We found the track more and more difficult to follow, and eventually had to abandon the struggle as the weather became threatening. We had climbed over 1000m up from the valley floor, and seen enough to warrant botanists returning for further study. It would make a fascinating trip to reach the Baurum Tso and then cross to Lachen, but would take about three days and involve camping on the way as the area is uninhabited.

The next two days were spoiled by almost continuous rain and low cloud, which made any trip into the mountains hazardous, so we used the time to walk the road along the valley to the north and south of Yumthang. The forest to the south still showed some of its summer glory, with a profusion of the pink orchid *Satyrium nepalense* and some fine clumps of *Primula capitata* ssp.*crispa*. This is one of my favourite primulas, with a tight head of drooping, dark mauve flowers and silver farina dusted all over the stem and flower stalks. Mohan found *Rhododendron roylei*

still in flower, another attractive species, with the backs of the red flowers covered in golden scales.

Pink *Bistorta amplexicaulis*, dark blue *Cynoglossum furcatum* and yellow *Saxifraga brachypoda*, grew all along the roadside, while *Goodyera repens* flourished wherever there was a good moss cover under the pine trees. Despite the rain, we managed to see a good representation of the forest birds, crested grey and crested black tits, Tickell's leaf-warblers and greenish warblers, Eurasian treecreepers, and in the more open areas by the river Blyth's pipits, white-capped and blue-fronted redstarts, stonechats, hoopoes and the ubiquitous white wagtails. A young Bonelli's eagle circled over us at one stop, and when we got back to Yumthang we could again hear the ibisbill, but they were hidden in the mist.

That evening Prakash brought me a large bat with long ears which had flown into the kitchen window and stunned itself. It had no broken bones, and after an hour wrapped in a warm cloth it emerged squeaking crossly and flew off.

White-capped redstart [Nigel Bean/Nature Picture Library]

At last, on 18th September, the weather improved and we took the jeep back to Yume Samdong, once more ascending the ridge into the Tembawa Chu. This time Siwa and I were determined to reach the valley head which I had briefly seen in 1996, so elected to go without lunch and push on as fast as we could. The valley is spectacular, with a flattish river bottom bounded on both sides by very steep jagged peaks. These are constantly eroding under the effects of snow and rain, with extensive screes spewing out onto the valley floor. In between these are the yak grazing meadows carpeted in flowers, each part of the valley separated by 200m tall banks of moraine debris running right across from one cliff side to the other. Three of these barriers have to be surmounted

Saussurea uniflora

Satyrium nepalense var.nepalense

Cremanthodium reniforme

Viola biflora

Tembawa Chu

before the valley swings abruptly north and terminates in massive ice cliffs.

On the scree slopes Mohan discovered hundreds of clumps of *Gentiana urnula* and mounds of several unidentifiable *Androsaces*. Near the valley head Siwa and I could hear Tibetan snowcock cackling high up on the slopes, audible but invisible. We reached the end of the valley with a dense mass of cloud creeping up behind us like a tide, filling the valley from side to side. Mohan was lower down underneath it, suffering snow and sleet, but the Rimpoche's blessing was with me and the sun appeared just long enough for me to take some photographs. Within two minutes the cloud engulfed us, and in driving snow we retreated. The walk back was hard, made worse by rain-soaked spectacles, which made it difficult to see my footing. We got lost in the mist, just as I had in 1996, and ended up with a long walk back to find

the bridge crossing which was invisible from above.

The Tembawa Chu valley is one of the most attractive and interesting of all the valleys of north Sikkim, and there is now a good chance that a scientific party will camp there for several days to study it. I also hope that they will rediscover the yellow *Cyananthus* I found there in 1996, which so far has not been identified.

We returned to Yumthang wet, exhausted and happy, to find a fire lit, while Gyapo had excelled himself and produced a magnificent supper. We all retired to our sleeping bags in a mellow frame of mind.

The next morning I was not alone in welcoming something a little less arduous, so we all piled into the jeep and drove down to Yakchey, just north of Lachung. On our drive up from Gangtok I had noticed flourishing colonies of *Satyrium nepalense* and *Primula capitata* in that area, but in the time we had been up country they had all passed their best and were no longer worth photographing. This was a mite disappointing, but, as we turned the jeep to drive back, we noticed a small side road running east. This led into the Damang valley, and it proved absolutely lovely. As you enter the valley Chuba Lhakang Gompa lies close to the road, a 200 year old temple of simple design. Its significance lies in the fact that a very important puja is held there every year, with the valley coming under the jurisdiction of the Lachung Gompa. There is a total ban on hunting or the cutting of trees in the valley, resulting in a gloriously unspoiled Himalayan forest such as I had not seen before in Sikkim. The sides of the valley rise nearly vertically, and on this particularly sunny day their pine clad cliffs, wreathed in

Rhodiola chrysanthemifolia

wisps of cloud, looked like a classical Chinese landscape painting.

We stopped for lunch among the trees by the river, where I found *Paris polyphylla* in fruit, with a cluster of red berries above the variegated foliage, yellow *Viola biflora*, *Swertia paniculata*, the small orchid *Herminium lanceum* and blue *Campanula aristata*. What really impressed me were the ancient gnarled forest trees, dripping with Spanish moss and covered in epiphytic flowers. A count on one old maple tree totalled fourteen species growing on the trunk and branches, including the orchid *Pleione hookeriana*, but most striking was the epiphyte *Rhodiola chrysanthemifolia*. Most rhodiolas have rather uninspiring yellow flowers and grow on rocks, but this beauty had big whorls of lobed, fleshy, red-flushed leaves like a bridal bouquet, at the centre of which sat a flat head of scarlet flowers. It was abundant in Damang valley, but we never saw it anywhere else. Forest birds, such as those we had seen at Yumthang, were everywhere, and our time in the Damang valley was all too short. I left with the conviction that this was how a Himalayan forest valley should be, and I

Damang Forest

Chuba Lhakang Gompa

Blood pheasant

Rula Chu and Chombu

can only pray that it will remain so.

Next day we took the opportunity to try to reach the icefalls and alpine slopes we could see across the valley from our bungalow camp. We crossed the river by the Yumthang hot springs and walked north until we came to the meadows which lay opposite Yumthang. They proved to be astonishingly rich, with thousands of small terrestrial orchids, *Herminium josephi, Aorchis spathulata*, and a few *Satyrium nepalense*. What surprised me was the profusion of *Gentiana ornata* growing at such a relatively low altitude.

At first the guides insisted that the path up through the forest, which I had seen on the old maps, no longer existed, but we persisted in our search and duly found the old track. It had not been used for about six years and in places was very overgrown, but it was well constructed and not difficult to follow.

The climb of 850m was steep and hard, with very few flowering plants to cheer us on our way, but we heard blood pheasants calling in the undergrowth and I briefly saw a male golden bush-robin. Finally we emerged above the forest trees and got a brief view of Yumthang down below before

it was completely obscured by swirling clouds.

Now we were faced by a dense belt of tangled rhododendron extending upwards for 350m, and sideways in both directions as far as the eye could see. Frustratingly close above us we could see the glacier gleaming in sunshine and the alpine slopes dotted with the big spikes of *Rheum nobile*, but our progress was desperately slow. By keeping to a ridge we managed to get some 100m higher up, but even there the bushes were head high and so tangled that one could scarcely squeeze through them or even under them. Finally we had to admit defeat and return downwards. It would have taken a small team with choppers several days to clear a route, which underlines the problem which exists throughout the Lachung valley of getting access to the heights where no tracks exist. Hooker had tried similarly to reach the glacier, and had also been forced to give up by the tangle. The only way to breach the belt of rhododendron is to work one's way up the scree chutes, which are steep and highly unstable.

Throughout our time in the north of Sikkim I had been praying for a chance to visit the country on the border with Tibet, and at last the weather relented with a glorious sunny, cloudless morning. The drive back up to Yume Samdong was a joy, with snowy peaks visible above us on all sides. and at last a clear view of Khangchengyao at the end of the valley above the hot springs. Zadong was reached, and we could appreciate the staggering panorama of high mountains which form the northern border of Sikkim. This was the old trade route to Lhasa along which the

caravans of yaks had passed in years gone by, the same route which the Younghusband Expedition had followed on its initial attempt to reach Lhasa in 1904. It was remarkable how quickly the track had become obscured, although substantial sections of stonework were still discernible.

We left the main track and followed a stream north-west into the valley of the Sangla Phu Tso. This is not a big lake, but it

Khangchengyao from Yume Samdong

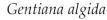
Gentiana algida

Gentiana urnula

IN THE VALLEY OF THE
SANGLA PHU TSO

Left: *Sanglaphu and Sanglaphu Tso*

Bottom left: *Gurudongmar from Sanglaphu Tso*

Below: *The east face of Gurondongmar*

is an absolute gem, set in a bowl with the perfect triangular peak of Sanglaphu rising behind it to the north. The lake waters were clear as crystal, bright blue in the sunshine, but devoid of any plant or animal life. The water is so cold for most of the year that nothing can live in it. Nearby the yak herders who use the high pastures in summer had erected a line of cairns. Towering above them to the west lay Gurudongmar, its east flank and summit glistening with a crown of ice. Vast icicles hung from the cliffs below overhanging bulges of snow, the whole ensemblage looking ready to cascade down at any minute. The silence was only broken by the trickle of water and the calls of a large flock of horned larks. Around the remains of a stone hut a family party of Daurian redstarts flitted, and scolded us for disturbing the peace.

We eventually had to move on from that enchanted place, carrying on round the contour of the mountain eastwards towards the Donkya La. The slopes were scarred by a series of screes, all of which were rich botanical hunting grounds. *Gentiana urnula* flourished, the flowers wide open in the sunshine, with a single group of late-flowering, pale blue *G.algida* and *G.ornata* in such profusion as I had never seen before anywhere in the eastern Himalaya. How often one hears the phrase 'colouring the ground' used to describe a particularly fine floral display, but here it was

literally true. It seemed a crime to walk through the flowers, but it was impossible to avoid treading on them. I found myself apologising to them for the intrusion!

Among the screes I discovered sheets of the little furry stars of*Leontopodium monocephalum* here in its white flowered form, hard cushions of *Arenaria bryophylla* studded with tiny white blooms, and large clumps of mauve flowered *Delphinium brunonianum*.

I had been intrigued, when looking at old geological maps of the valley south of the Donkya Ri, to see a site described by Hooker as 'Fossil limestone much folded and faulted'. Limestone of any sort is rare in

Delphinium brunonianum

Sheets of Gentiana ornata south of the Donkya La

Our team at the roadhead, Zadong. Left to right: Prakash, Kumar, driver, Sonam, Mohan, Yamphel and Ganden

The old traders' route to the Donkya La

the eastern Himalaya, an example being the famous 'yellow band' below the summit of Everest. All are relics of the bed of the ancient Tethys Sea, upheaved as the Himalaya rose, but most of the limestone has long since eroded away. There was always the hope that an area might remain and serve as a niche for calcicole plants, and these could be very interesting indeed. Eventually I located the site, a tall triangular cliff 200m high crossed by clearly marked strata, and completely different in colour to all the surrounding area. However, it was surrounded by a permanent snowfield, while the valley slopes around comprised shattered rock, dry and desolate – no chance of finding the plants I had hoped might grow there. After a final look to the snowy Donkya La, we had to turn back down the valley as the light faded on a perfect day.

Earlier in the trip we had been thwarted in our efforts to reach the icefalls and glaciers east of Yumthang, which we could see so clearly across the river. Behind us to the west the mountains rose very steeply to a line of jagged black peaks, which were usually shrouded in cloud. On my previous visit I had eyed them with interest and wondered just what lay on the other side. No one could tell me, and it seemed that few had ever been there since the mountains offered nothing for grazing stock, lacked any tracks and ranged from very steep to well nigh vertical. They did have one advantage, however. The zone of impenetrable rhododendron was breached in several places by stone chutes, one of which stretched up over 1300m from behind our camp into the clouds.

We made an early start and were soon scrambling up a 45° slope littered with loose stones and large boulders. As is so often the case in such unstable terrain, large plants such as rhododendron cannot maintain a roothold, and the small alpines can flourish without being crowded out. We soon found *Geranium nakaonum* which we had not seen before, with the gorgeous big pink flowers of *Pedicularis megalantha* and its taller, darker relative *P.roylei*. We also flushed three female Impeyan pheasants, which rocketed off and vanished in the scrub bordering the gully.

The slope began to steepen and we were forced to cross and recross the stone chutes to try to gain altitude up grass covered ridges. There I found the yellow *Delphinium viscosum* we had encountered up the Sewken Chu, tiny dark blue *Gentianella stellariifolia* and an unidentifiable white saxifrage. This was a most unusual looking type, the edges of the lower half of each petal being deeply frilled.

We had now reached the steepest part of the climb, where the gully forked and the gradient steepened to 70°. The right hand route was blocked by huge boulders, so we clawed our way up to the left. Giant rhubarb now put in an appearance, with a white buttercup similar to *Ranunculus glacialis* and mats of yellow *Potentilla eriocarpa* on the cliff face. So far the weather had stayed dry, but Ganden was rightly concerned that any rain would make our descent hazardous. Siwa had pressed on

Delphinium viscosum

Cremanthodium palmatum

The route above Yumthang

Silene nigrescens

Summit at 6000m above Yumthang

ahead, and we could make out a tiny figure on the skyline exultantly waving his arms. This was all the excuse I needed to push on, and we reached the top after a climb of four hours.

The view was breathtaking. Below us lay a bowl-shaped cwm with a lake at the bottom, ringed by pinnacles and rocks like jagged teeth. It was one of the most fiercely wild looking places I have ever seen in the mountains, and cried out for more time to be spent exploring it. It does not appear on any of the maps, and our local guide Sonam felt that it had seldom been visited, certainly not by a westerner. We sat and waited for a break in the mist so that I could take a

photograph, and then began the tricky descent. This was every bit as difficult as we had anticipated, and all of us slipped several times, but suffered nothing worse than muddy trousers. We flushed several more impeyan on the way down, including a fine colourful male, and near the bottom of the scree I found a patch of *Silene nigrescens*, each attractive flower like a little hanging lampshade with ribs of purple velvet.

Next day started wet, but after a while it cleared enough for us to explore the meadows more fully on the east side of the river opposite the Yumthang bungalow. In addition to the masses of terrestrial orchids

Lakes and peaks west of the summit

we had already found there we found plenty of *Goodyera fusca* growing out of clumps of dwarf *Rhododendron setosum*, while on the edge of the meadows where the forest began I found plenty of *Goodyera repens* and a single spike of *Listera pinetorum*. More exciting were two considerable colonies of *Malaxis acuminata*, identifiable but past their best. This was late September, and one can only guess what a picture these meadows would be in June and July. We had been unable to see them at that time in 1996 when we were in Yumthang, as all the bridges had been swept away by the flood of 1994.

Along the edges of the river gravels *Myricaria rosea* was just starting to develop the lovely reddish tints of autumn foliage. Under the larger forest rhododendrons the sinister looking spikes of the parasitic plant *Xylanche himalaica* were abundant. The river meadows were excellent for bird life, and we saw ibisbill with half grown young, white-capped redstarts, Blyth's pipits,

Yumthang valley

Tickell's leaf-warblers, hoopoes, and stonechats. There is no doubt in my mind that Yumthang makes a most excellent centre for exploring the Lachung valley, which has so much more to offer than we were able to see in the time we were there.

This was our last evening at Yumthang, and I was having my supper on my own, as Mohan had departed for Gangtok earlier in the day. I was aware suddenly of shuffling feet and giggling outside the door of my room, the doors were flung open, and there in the candlelight were all the staff with the cook Gyapo bearing a magnificent cake. The iced top bore the message 'David Many More Happy Plant Years!' This was typical of the kindness which I had so much enjoyed throughout the trip.

At last the time had arrived to return to civilisation, and we made an uneventful journey back to Gangtok. The next few days were fully taken up with meetings and discussions on what we had recorded in the north, and in enjoying the generous hospitality of my kind friends. At last also we caught up on world news and learned much of the detail of the horrors of the September 11 terrorist attack on New York. The prospect of the return flight home over Afghanistan was not reassuring, but proved in the end to be trouble free.

It felt bizarre to learn of all the angst and hatred that seemed to be overwhelming the rest of the world, while for a month I, a stranger, had been treated with such universal kindness in a country not my own.

Postlude

Yet each man kills the thing he loves,
By each let this be heard.

Oscar Wilde: 'The Ballad of Reading Gaol'

Cleome speciosa

It could be argued, with some degree of fairness, that in writing such a book as this I am focusing attention on an environment which is fragile and precious, and that this could be to its detriment. I would argue that if we do not understand something properly we cannot value it as we should.

I have come to love Sikkim deeply, and I am apprehensive for the future, so what I say here is said in that spirit and not in the spirit of criticism. I have spent a lifetime studying flowers and wildlife, and for many years I have been actively involved in nature conservation, so that I am well aware of the problems which we all face, whatever country we live in.

At a county biological recorders' seminar in Sussex, which I attended in the spring of 2000, one speaker made the point that successful conservation depends upon good records of wildlife. The records in their turn depend upon successful conservation actions, otherwise there would be nothing worthwhile left to record. It seems so obvious, and yet the implementation of the concept is fraught with difficulty. In Great Britain we are fortunate in having a vast collection of biological data stretching back, in some cases, for centuries, and a large body of amateur and professional experts dedicated to the study of nature. Despite this, we still have immense conservation problems, and in so many areas we appear to be losing the battle against the opposing forces of money, development and political indifference.

No one would deny that Sikkim is small, but it possesses priceless riches of natural habitat, birds, wild animals and above all

The glorious Damang valley

Gentiana urnula

Near the Donkya La

wild flowers. Instinctively the naturalist wants to keep these wonders unspoiled, but is hampered by lack of detailed knowledge of what is there. The first priority must surely be to create an accessible and comprehensive record of what exists now, for, as is the case in Britain, conservation decisions cannot be made in a vacuum of knowledge. Yet there is an urgent need to make informed decisions while there is still time and before too much is lost. Some of these decisions may well seem unpalatable now, but a long-term view must be cultivated which is for the greater good of Sikkim.

The development of the tourist industry in a small country with limited natural resources is rightly viewed as an essential ingredient in the well-being of the state, but tourism makes immense demands on the whole infrastructure and can overwhelm it if it is not managed with great care. If we rigidly control tourist access we are accused of operating an exclusive policy and being elitist. If on the other hand an uncontrolled flood of tourists is permitted then, as experience has shown in other countries, it debases the very amenities they have come to see, so that the country no longer attracts the tourism it was trying to cultivate. It needs the wisdom of a present day Solomon to balance these seemingly irreconcilable demands, which are aggravated by increasing demands for living space and improved living standards for an expanding population.

I feel that such knowledge does exist today within Sikkim, but that there is a price to pay to harness that knowledge, both monetarily and in the realm of political will. The vision has got to be long term – not just five years ahead, but fifty years, when many of us will no longer be here. As someone in Gangtok drily remarked to me, 'There aren't many votes in that!'

If this book opens people's eyes to the wonders of the flowers and wildlife of Sikkim, and encourages tourists to come with a proper respect for what it offers, then I shall be well content.

Floreat Sikkim!

Forest Orchids of Sikkim

by Mohan Pradhan

Between China and the kingdoms of Nepal and Bhutan lies Sikkim, a landscape set between the third highest peak in the world – Khangchendzonga (8603m) – and the low inland valleys, with a unique biosphere ranging from tropical to alpine within the brief north to south distance of scarcely 150km. Sikkim has been called 'The botanist's paradise', an apt name, as the country possesses immeasurable riches in biodiversity, with over 4000 species of flowering plants within an area of 7300 square kilometres.

Among these flowering plants orchids have a special significance, making the region of international importance. In Sikkim the earliest record of an orchid

At present approximately 495 species of orchid representing 110 genera are found in Sikkim Himalaya. The following eight genera are dominant, accounting for almost 40 per cent of the total:

Bulbophyllum (45 species)
Dendrobium (36 species)
Liparis (22 species)
Eria (22 species)
Oberonia (21 species)
Cymbidium (16 species)
Calanthe (16 species)
Coelogyne (12 species)

collection is that made by W. Griffith in 1843. Sir Joseph Hooker collected extensively in Sikkim between 1849 and 1851, and published the results in *The Flora of British India* Vol V & VI (1885) and *Icones Plantarum* (1890). King and Pantling published an exclusive illustrated work in 1898 containing 448 species representing 91 genera.

Orchid Habitat

In the Sikkim Himalaya there are four major habitat zones, which are by no means exclusive, as some orchid species will be found in more than one zone. The four zones are:
1. Tropical (250–800m)
2. Sub-tropical (800–1800m)
3. Sub-temperate to temperate (1800– 3500m)
4. Alpine (above 3500m)
Forest orchids are found in the first three zones up to an altitude of 3500m.

Phalaenopsis mannii

Paphiopedilum venustum

1. Tropical zone

This is characterized by dense forest, mainly of *Mangifera*, *Ficus*, *Shorea*, *Cassia*, *Bombax*, *Artocarpus* and other species, with a secondary vegetation of bamboo and palms. Summer temperatures range from 30°–38°C by day to 20°–27°C by night, while in the winter the night time temperatures can drop to 10°C. Within the

zone orchids will be found in the following habitats:

a) Trees. *Ascocentrum ampullaceum, Cymbidium aloifolium, Dendrobium jenkinsii, D.formosum* and numerous other species.

b) Secondary vegetation. *Bulbophyllum* species, *Eria* species, *Phalaenopsis mannii* and *P.lobbii.*

c) River banks. *Anoectochilus roxburghii,* other 'jewel orchid' species, *Calanthe* species.

d) Sandstone outcrops and cliffs. *Diplomeris hirsuta, Arundina graminifolia, Eulophia* and *Habenaria* species.

2. *Sub-tropical zone*

This zone is mostly composed of mixed deciduous and evergreen forests. The dominant trees are *Quercus, Prunus, Magnolia, Schima, Alnus, Bauhinia* and *Leucosceptrum.* Summer temperatures range from 25°–32°C by day to 10°–15°C by night. This zone experiences heavy rainfall (800–

2000mm) during the monsoon period when most orchids grow rapidly and complete their annual growth. During the winters, which are cool and dry, the plants draw water from the occasional rain and nightly condensation. Orchids occupy the following habitats:

a) Trees. *Bulbophyllum* species, *Esmeralda cathcartii, Cymbidium* species, *Oberonia* species, *Pleione maculata* etc.

b) Bamboo and palm thickets. *Paphiopedilum venustum, Eulophia* species, *Calanthe* and *Phaius* species.

c) Forest floor. *Cymbidium lancifolium, Phaius, Anoectochilus* and *Habenaria* species

d) Rock faces. *Paphiopedilum fairreanum* on grassy ledges, *Anthiogonum gracile* and *Habenaria* species where it is muddy, and *Bulbophyllum leopardinum* on steep rocks.

3 *Sub-temperate to temperate*

This zone experiences snow in the cooler

Below, left to right:
Phalaenopsis lobbii
Esmeralda cathcartii
Rhyncostylis retusa

months of the year, and is characterised by mist at all times of the year. The dominant vegetation consists of *Alnus, Acer, Abies, Pinus, Larix, Quercus, Magnolia* and *Rhododendron*. The summer temperature varies from 18°–21°C by day to 10°–15°C by night, and during the winter reaches 10°C by day, while it is often below freezing at night. Rainfall is at a peak from June to September, thereafter decreasing rapidly. Orchids occupy the following habitats:

a) Trees. *Cymbidium grandiflorum, C.elegans, Coelogyne cristata, Pleione hookeriana, Dendrobium candidum, D.hookerianum* and *Vanda undulata.*

b) Forest floor. *Goodyera fusca,* the 'jewel orchids', *Calanthe chloroleuca* and *Nervillea macroglossa.*

c) Grassy slopes. *Habenaria* species, *Liparis* species, *Satyrium nepalense* etc.

d) Rocky outcrops. *Pleione humilis, Satyrium nepalense, Anthogonium gracile* and *Spathoglottis ixioides.*

The following brief descriptions highlight some of the more beautiful orchids that occur in Sikkim, especially those in genera which are well represented across the country.

Bulbophyllum This large and diverse genus is represented by no fewer than 45 species. In the tropical zone *Bulbophyllum putidum* (*B.ornatissimum*) grows as an epiphyte on trees, and has the longest flowers of its genus (10–18cm). *B.helenae* is another epiphyte, with masses of orange-red flowers. In the sub-tropical zone *B.sikkimense* with greenish-white flowers and *B.wallichii* with fragrant pale green flowers also grow on trees. *B.leopardinum* grows in large colonies on moss-covered

rocks, each plant carrying 1–3 large pale yellow flowers spotted with crimson. In the sub-temperate zone *B.viridifolium* is a deciduous species with racemes up to 10cm long of vivid green flowers.

Dendrobium This genus is one of the most flamboyant of all the orchids of the Sikkim Himalaya. In the tropical zone grows *Dendrobium formosum* with large, fragrant white flowers, and *D.fimbriatum* with 1 metre-tall canes bearing orange-yellow flowers. In the sub-tropical zone *D.aphyllum* with pale, mauvish-pink flowers grows abundantly on trees, with *D.densiflorum* whose flower spikes have a fanciful resemblance to a bunch of bananas. Here also grows the national flower of Sikkim, *D.nobile*, with mauve-tipped petals and a stunning blackish-purple 'eye' at the base of the lip. The summer flowering species *D.chrysanthum* is widely distributed in the sub-tropical and sub-temperate zones, growing on both trees and rocks, and is a common sight on the edge of Gangtok.

Dendrobium nobile

Cymbidium devonianum

Anoectochilus brevilabris

Coelogyne nitida

Another summer flowering species is *D.hookerianum*, a rare species with beautiful large yellow flowers, the lip margin heavily fimbriated. White-flowered *D.candidum* can be found growing both on rocks and on the branches of rhododendrons.

Cymbidium Sixteen species have been recorded in Sikkim. *Cymbidium munroianum*, with fragrant, straw-coloured flowers, grows in the tropical zone, with *C.ensifolium* and *C.aloifolium*, an epiphyte which produces large masses of buff coloured flowers in summer. In the sub-tropical zone *C.lancifolium* grows in deep, rich humus on the forest floor, its long cigar-shaped pseudobulbs being diagnostic. There also grows *C.eburneum* with fragrant ivory-white flowers and *C.cochleare* with metallic brown flowers. *C.whiteae* is an epiphytic rarity with green flowers heavily spotted with purplish-red, whose extremely limited habitat is under threat. *C.elegans*, with pendulous pale flowers, and *C.devonianum* with drooping brown flowers tipped with pink, both flower in the spring in the sub-temperate zone. Another spring flowering species is the epiphyte *C.grandiflora*, with large apple-green flowers.

Coelogyne The species within this genus are found growing as epiphytes or lithophytes on moss covered rocks and cliffs. *Coelogyne treutleri* has been seen only once, in the tropical zone. In the sub-tropical zone *C.flavida* with small yellow flowers, *C.nitida* with fragrant white flowers and *C.fuscescens* with large yellow-brown flowers, are all found on rocks and trees. In the sub-temperate zone *C.cristata* grows in large, impressive clumps producing pendulous spikes of large, pure white flowers marked with orange. The most bizarre species, growing in the cool temperate zone, is *C.barbata*, the large white flowers having a lip bearded in blackish-brown.

Calanthe This is a fine group of mostly winter flowering orchids. They all have soft, pleated leaves, and are terrestrial or lithophytes, rarely growing as epiphytes. *Calanthe alismaefolia* with pale greenish-white flowers and *C.masuca* with a dense inflorescence of purple-lilac flowers are both widely distributed in the tropical zone. *C.biloba* of the sub-tropical zone has long racemes of more than sixty yellow flowers, mottled with violet-brown.

Also found in this zone, although its range extends into the sub-temperate zone, is *C.tricarinata*, the yellow-green flowers having a lip bearing red-brown ridges. *C.whiteana* with densely flowered racemes of yellow flowers is extremely rare, and was recently rediscovered after more than half a century. A Sikkimese endemic species found in the deep shade of primary forest is *C.chloroleuca*, which has very ornamental, fragrant yellow-green flowers in spikes up to 30cm long.

Pleione All of the four species found in Sikkim are dwarf plants with deciduous foliage, and grow on moss covered rocks and trees. *Pleione maculata* has fragrant white flowers and grows in the sub-tropical zone. *P.humilis* of the sub-temperate zone has white flowers mottled with brown spots. Another resident of this zone is the impressive *P.praecox*, which produces deep violet-rose to pink flowers in autumn. *P.hookeriana* grows in the temperate zone and above, growing on moss-covered branches and rocks, the pseudobulbs often totally embedded in the moss. It produces a profusion of pinkish-white flowers in spring.

The Jewel Orchids These form what is probably the most exquisite group of orchids, having beautifully patterned leaves. They grow in shady areas with high humidity, as terrestrials or lithophytes, rarely as epiphytes. Widely distributed in the tropical zone is *Anoectochilus roxburghii*, which has very ornamental chocolate to bronze-black leaves, netted with gold veins. The creeping *Goodyera hispida* produces dark bluish-green leaves with dense white veins. In the sub-tropical zone grows *Odontochilus elwesii* which has bluish-green leaves with an almost metallic sheen. Also in this zone grows *Zeuxine abbreviata* whose leaves bear a large white central vein and *Anoectochilus brevilabris* with broad velvety, maroon-garnet coloured leaves netted in pale gold. On the floor of the cool, wet temperate forests one can find *Goodyera hemsleyana* with silver reticulated dark leaves and *Odontochilus lanceolatus*, probably the showiest of the group, with white veined leaves and apple-green flowers bearing a prominent deep yellow lip.

Vandaceous Orchids Most of the species of this diverse group grow as epiphytes, or less commonly as lithophytes, being found from the tropical to the sub-temperate zones. In the tropical zone *Paplioanthe teres* is common and widely distributed, producing large colonies of tall flower spikes covered with large rose-purple flowers. *Aerides multiflorum*, a common spring-flowering species, grows on trees where it forms large pendulous spikes of dozens of tiny pink and white flowers marked with purple spots. In the same habitat one can find *Rhyncostylis retusa*, a handsome species, bearing fragrant spikes of pink and white flowers in spring. *Gastrochilus dasypogon*, a dwarf species with bright yellow flowers, is also found in this zone, where it grows in deep shade on secondary vegetation. *Ascocentrum ampullaceum* grows on exposed tree trunks in both the tropical and sub-tropical zones. A dwarf species, *Acampe papillosa* is very widespread, growing on exposed rocks and trees where it forms very large masses covered with pinkish-purple flowers. *Esmeralda cathcartii* is a highly ornamental species which grows in deep shade, in cool forest glades by streams, often with *E.clarkei*, both forming large, straggly masses, the latter having flowers with rather narrow segments The fleshy, round flowers of *E.cathcartii*, 5–8cm in diameter, are white outside and finely barred with chocolate-brown within. *Vanda undulata* grows on moss laden trees in the temperate zone, having fragrant, pink-flushed white flowers. There also grows *Uncifera obtusifolia*, a delightful miniature species with pendulous yellow flowers. *Vanda cristata* is a spring flowering, miniature species of the sub-tropical zone. The flowers are green with a brown lip which bears two horns, giving it the name of 'dragon-tongued orchid'.

Vanda undulata

Nephelaphyllum pulchrum var.*sikkimensis*

Paphiopedilum fairreanum

Other interesting orchid species In the tropical zone *Arundina graminifolia* is common on open grassy slopes and mud banks. It is a very ornamental species with a growth form like a small bamboo 2–3m high, and it is sometimes grown as a simple garden hedge. The flowers are large and showy, white to deep rose in colour, resembling a *Cattleya*. In similar habitat grows *Eulophia zollingeri*, a terrestrial species bearing beautiful brown-red flowers on scapes 20 – 60cm tall. With these grow *Phaius tankervilliae*, a plant of bamboo thickets, with striking flowers of brown to rose-pink, and *P.flavus* with yellow flowers and ornamental yellow-spotted leaves. *Diplomeris hirsuta* is a deciduous species found growing on steep banks in the tropical zone, bearing beautiful miniature white flowers in summer. On the forest floors of the tropical zone grow *Nephelaphyllum pulchrum* var.*sikkimensis*, a terrestrial species with fleshy, copper coloured leaves mottled with purple, and *Tainia wrayana*, with fleshy, heart-shaped leaves and brown flowers. In the sub-tropical zone *Eria bambusifolia* is found growing on trees and *E coronaria* is found similarly on moss-laden rocks, growing well up into the sub-temperate zone. Both the *Paphiopedilum* species which occur in Sikkim will be found here. *P.fairreanum* grows on steep ledges amidst grasses, having beautiful white flowers veined with purple and green. *P.venustum* grows on shady banks in bamboo and palm thickets, and has handsomely mottled leaves. In the sub-temperate and temperate zones *Habenaria pectinata* grows on grassy slopes and open shady embankments on the edge of forests. It produces greenish-white flowers with a distinctive three-lobed lip, the side lobes deeply cut so that they resemble a stag's antlers. Also in this zone grows *Spathoglottis ixioides*, the only cool growing member of its genus. It usually grows on grassy banks or on moss covered rocky outcrops, producing beautiful deep yellow flowers.

The future This unique group of plants has played an important part in the exploration of Sikkim, and its exposure to botanical study. The 495 species represent nearly 40 per cent of all the species found in India, a significant number when one considers the relative size of Sikkim. Further monographic and revisionary studies will necessitate a revised number in the future. During the past two decades the Sikkim Himalaya have witnessed large scale development, which has resulted in extensive habitat destruction and a decline in the diversity of the forest vegetation. Orchids in particular have suffered, as they are usually the most sensitive to a change in the ecological balance, and are the first to disappear. Already we have lost species such as *Coelogyne treutleri*, and are close to losing the tiny populations of *Paphiopedilum fairreanum*, *P.venustum*, *Calanthe whiteana* and *Cymbidium whiteae*. Construction of roads and the clearing of forests all take their toll of orchid species, both in numbers and diversity. There is a special urgency to protect and safeguard habitat where new, and as yet unknown, species may still await discovery.

Glossary

Agag: King of Amalek (I Samuel v16)
Atta: wheat flour
Ayah: children's nurse
A-yu: polled yak breed

Ban-jagri: type of small yeti (Nepali for 'wild witch doctor')
Bharal: blue sheep (*Pseudonis nayaur*)
Bhotia: ethnic group originating in Tibet
Bhutia: see Bhotia
Bod-gyag: small breed of yak

Chait: a memorial structure
Chang: millet beer
Cheng: hard dried cheese, sold in squares
Chogyal: hereditary ruler of Sikkim
Choiga: yak cheese
Chorten: a memorial structure
Chowkidar: caretaker
Chu: stream or river (Tibetan)
Chungku: wild dog (Tibetan for 'single hunter')
Cwm: deep bowl-shaped valley (Welsh)

Dak: government bungalow for travellers
Deciduous: having leaves which fall in autumn
Dewan: appointed Prime-minister
Dorji: religious instrument, thunderbolt of Indra
Drukpa Tseshi: festival to celebrate first teachings of the Buddha
Dungpa: official in charge of an administrative area
Dzo: hybrid between bull yak and female cow or buffalo
Dzo-mu: female of the hybrid
Dzong: fortress
Dzong-pen: official in charge of a dzong
Dzonka: language of Bhutan, of Tibetan origin

Epiphyte: plant growing on the surface of another

Fimbriated: bordered with hairs

Gelukpa: the dominant Bhuddist sect, reformed in the 14th century
Gid: disease of cattle and sheep caused by tapeworm cyst in brain
Gneiss: hard laminated rock of quartz, feldspar and mica
Gompa: religious building, both temple and monastery
Gure: purified butter

Harayan: member of low Indian caste

Jingal: 19th Century muzzle-loading gun used by Tibetan army

Kata: ceremonial silk scarf
Keratoconjunctivitis: inflammation of the superficial structures of the eye
Khang: area of permanent snow (Tibetan)
Kiang: Tibetan wild ass
Kukri: curved knife used by the Gurkhas

La: a pass (Tibetan)
Lama: a Bhuddist monk in holy orders
Lepcha: aboriginal inhabitant of Sikkim
Lho-gyap: large yak breed peculiar to Sikkim
Lithophyte: plant growing on rocks
Liver-fluke: internal trematode parasite of genus *Fasciola*

Mahayana doctrine: theistic and metaphysical form of Buddhism introduced by the monk Asvagosha
Mani wall: a wall built of mani stones inscribed with the prayer 'Om Mani Padme Hum'
Marco Polo sheep: wild sheep *Ovis ammon* ssp.*hodgsonii*
Megyoi: a type of yeti (Tibetan)
Mendong: a memorial structure

Nepali: a native of Nepal

Nyan: local name for Marco Polo sheep

Nyingmapa: the old Buddhist sect unreformed in the 14th century

Pipon: elected village head, as in Lachung and Lachen

Puja: a religious ceremony seeking blessing

Purdah: Indian system of the seclusion of women

Raceme: an inflorescence with flowers opening in sequence from the base

Raja: an hereditary prince or king

Rakshi: spirit distilled from fermented grains

Rang: a stream (Lepcha)

Rhakdong: long ceremonial trumpets

Ri: a mountain (Tibetan)

Rimpoche: a re-incarnation

Rinderpest: infectious disease of ruminants

Sal: an important commercial timber tree (*Shorea robusta*)

Sangtrolpalri: an intricate tiered representation of the different levels of Buddhist heaven and hell

Scape: the flowering stem of a plant on which all the leaves are basal

Shieling: summer hill grazing away from main farm (Scots)

Sirdar: senior member of camping staff

Stupa: memorial shrine, not necessarily containing relics

Takchu: yak cheese

Takin: wild goat-sheep species (*Budorcas taxicolor*)

Terai: sub-tropical area between the plains and the mountains

Thang: a meadow (Tibetan)

Thanka: a religious painting or hanging

Tso: a lake (Tibetan)

Yak: wild or domesticated ruminant (*Bos grunniens*)

Alternative Place-names

Visitors to Sikkim may find difficulty with multiple, alternative spellings of place-names, according to the map consulted. I have been advised in Sikkim to follow the spelling used in a map 'The Kingdom of Sikkim' by Pradyumna Pradhan (University of Kentucky 1969). The most commonly used alternative is given afterwards, in brackets.

Bakkhim (Bakhim)
Baurum Tso (Barum Chho)
Bikhbari (Bikbari)
Chu (Chhu)
Goecha La (Goeche La)
Jhopunu (Japanu)
Kabur (Kabru)
Khang (Kang)
Khangchendzonga (Kanchenjunga)
Khangchengyao (Kangchengyao)
Likship (Legship)
Meyong Chu (Mayan Chu)
Onglakthang (Onglathang)

Phalung (Phaklung)
Phithang (Phedang)
Phune (Puni)
Rangka (Rangkha)
Rangphu (Rangpo)
Rathong (Ratong)
Sang La Phu Tso (Sanglapu Cho)
Say-Say La (SeSe La)
Singhik (Singik)
Tista (Teesta)
Thanggu (Thangku)
Thay La (The La)
Tso (Chho or Cho)
Tsokha (Choka)
Tsomgo (Chomgo)
Tsoptah (Tchopta)
Tsunthang (Chungtang)
Tung (Toong)
Yachey (Yakshe)
Yuksam (Yoksum)
Yumthang (Yumtang)
Zemathang (Chemathang)

The following are some translations of commonly used place names:

Chomolhari: The hill of the lady goddess
Donkya La: Pass where even the wild yak are frozen
Gangtok: The high or level-topped hill
Jelep La: The level or easy pass
Khangchendzonga: Great snow of the five treasures (or five peaks)
Khangchengyao: The bearded kanchin – due to large ice-fall on the south face
Lachen: The big pass
Lachung: The little pass
Natu La: the pass of the listening ear
Samdong: The place for a bridge
Sebu La: The cold pass
Singale (Singli) La: Pass of the wild alder
Yuksam (Yoksum): Meeting place of three lamas

Bibliography

Ali,S. (1962) *The Birds of Sikkim* (Oxford University Press)
(1977) *Field Guide to the Birds of the Eastern Himalaya*
(Oxford University Press)
(1979) *The Book of Indian Birds* (Bombay Natural History Soc)

Bor,E. (1952) *Adventures of a Botanist's Wife* (Hurst & Blackett)

Fleming,P. (1962) *Bayonets to Lhasa* (Rupert Hart-Davis)

Fleming,R.L.Senr., Fleming R.L.Junr., and Bangdel,L.S.
(1976) *Birds of Nepal* (Avalok Pub.)

Freeman-Attwood,J. (1998) *The British Sikkim Expedition 1996.*
The Alpine Journal

Green,R. (1976) *Asiatic Primulas* (The Alpine Garden Society)

Grewal,B. and Pfister,O. (1998) *A Photographic Guide to
Birds of the Himalaya* (New Holland Publishers (UK)Ltd)

Grierson,A.J.C. and Long,D.G. (1983) *Flora of Bhutan –
including a record of plants from Sikkim. I (1)*
(Royal Botanic Garden Edinburgh)
(1984) *Flora of Bhutan – including a record of plants
from Sikkim I (2)* (Royal Botanic Garden Edinburgh)
(1987) *Flora of Bhutan – including a record of plants
from Sikkim I (3)* (Royal Botanic Garden Edinburgh)
(1991) *Flora of Bhutan 2 (1)* (Royal Botanic Garden Edinburgh)
(1999) *Flora of Bhutan – including a record of plants
from Sikkim and Darjeeling 2 (2)* (Royal Botanic
Garden Edinburgh and Royal Government of Bhutan)

Haribal,M. (1992) *The Butterflies of Sikkim Himalaya*
(Sikkim Nature Conservation Foundation)

Harrer,H. (1953) *Seven Years in Tibet* – translated by
Richard Graves. (Rupert Hart-Davis)

Hooker,Sir.J.D. (1854) *Himalayan Journals; or Notes of a
Naturalist in Bengal, the Sikhim and Nepal Mountains, Etc.,*
(Murray)

Inskipp,C. (1989) *Nepal's Forest Birds: their status and
conservation* (International Council for Bird
Preservation)

Inskipp,C. and Inskipp,T.(1991) *A guide to the Birds of Nepal*
(Christopher Helm Ltd)

Inskipp,C. Inskipp,T. and Grimmett.R. (1999) *Birds of
Bhutan* 2nd.edition (Oxford University Press)

Jack,A. (1938) *Tibetan Diary 4.8.1938–16.10.1938*
(manuscript)

Long,D.G. (1989) *Notes Relating to the Flora of Bhutan*:
XIII Ericaceae Notes R.B.G. Edinburgh 45(2):227-335

Noltie,H.J. (1994) *Flora of Bhutan – including a record of
plants from Sikkim and Darjeeling 3 (1)* (Royal Botanic
Garden Edinburgh)

Pang-Lhab-Sol (2001) *Celebration Committee Souvenirs*
(Himadri Printers Gangtok)

Pearce,N.R and Cribb,P.J (2002) *Flora of Bhutan 3 (3) The
Orchids of Bhutan* (Royal Botanic Garden Edinburgh)

Perry,A (1949) *Kalimpong and the Sikkim Hills* (Tibet Mirror
Press, Kalimpomg)

Polunin,O and Stainton,A (1984) *Flowers of the Himalaya*
(Oxford University Press)

Risley,H.H et al (1994) *The Gazeteer of Sikhim* (Sikkim
Nature Conservation Foundation)

Rustomji,N (1971) *Enchanted Frontiers: Sikkim, Bhutan and
India's North-eastern Borderlands* (Oxford University
Press London)
(1978) Bhutan: *The Dragon Kingdom in Crisis* (Oxford
University Press London)

Shepheard,K (1938) *Tibetan Diary 4.8.1938–16.10.1938*
(manuscript)

Shukla,B.K., Singh,P and Chauhan,A.S (1998) *Orchid
Diversity in Sikkim and its Conservation* J.Orchid
Soc.India 12(1-2):53-76

Stainton,A (1988) *Flowers of the Himalaya* – a Supplement
(Oxford University Press)

Stevens, H (1992) *Birds, Discovery and Conservation.*
Edit.David Snow Report on expedition 28.12.1930–21.4.1931
collecting bird specimens *Annals of British Ornithologists
Club* (Helm Information)

Tenzing,D (1986) *Coenurosis in Yak in Bhutan*
(Animal Husbandry Department Thimphu)

Whistler,H (1941) *Popular Handbook of
Indian Birds* (Gurney and Jackson)

Younghusband,Sir.F (1910) *India and Tibet* (London)

Acknowledgements

I am acutely aware that, in writing a book which covers a period of more than 17 years, it is all too easy to forget the help one has received from different individuals. So, if I have omitted to thank anyone, the fault is mine alone, and I shall plead mitigation by reason of age.

My thanks are due to the following:

Dr Phillip Cribb, Deputy Director of the Herbarium, Royal Botanic Gardens, Kew, and to Marilyn Ward, Illustrations Curator, Kew, for tracing and supplying copies of paintings made by Sir Joseph Hooker in 1849.

Dr David Long and Dr Henry Noltie of Royal Botanic Garden, Edinburgh, for their companionship in Sikkim, and for their technical advice.

John Sparks, former head of BBC Natural History Unit, Bristol, for his help and advice, and Laura Goodchild of the BBC Nature Picture Library, Bristol, for tracing specific wildlife slides for this book.

Patricia Rogers of Pestalozzi Village, Sedlescombe, for permission to copy photographs taken by her father, Lt Ken Shepheard on his journey through Sikkim to Tibet in 1938.

Sir Edward Peck GCMG, for the photograph of Jitsu Drake taken during our trek to Bhutan in 1985.

Robin Pepper, Jean Petrie and Simon Lingington for their help in the tedious job of scrutinising text, and for their advice, which I have tried to follow.

Keith Wilson, for expert help and advice on photographic problems.

In Sikkim I am particularly grateful to Tashi Tobden, Additional Chief Secretary, Government of Sikkim, for his permission to copy photographs from his family archive, for detailed advice on the text and the correct spelling of place-names.

Wangyal Tobden, Rajesh Lakhotia and Lekshed Gyaltshen, my trekking companions in 1989, for all their help and friendship to an eccentric foreigner.

Ganden and Usha Lachungpa of Atlas Tours, for companionship on trek and for their efficient organisation, which catered so well for our needs.

I am most grateful to my friend Mohan Pradhan for writing the special chapter on the forest orchids of Sikkim, and for the use of his splendid colour slides to illustrate it.

To all my good friends in Britain and Sikkim, my heartfelt thanks. I hope you will find this book some reward for all your help and kindness over the years.

The following are personnel involved with the four expeditions in Sikkim, and their roles:

The Delectable Mountains
(24.4.1987–15.5.1987)
David Lang
Peter Hoggarth
Rosamund Hoggarth
Helen Proctor
Gladys Sellers
Bimal Kanta Rai (external guide)
Dharmey Tenzing Norgay (sirdar)
Karma (assistant)
Ombhadur Chettri (assistant)
Pasang (cook)
Pasang (cook boy)

Against the Odds
(21.6.1989–12.7.1989)
Wangyal Tobden
Rajesh Lakhotia
Lekshed Gyaltshen
David Lang
Ashun (cook)

In the Steps of Hooker
(2.7.1996–31.7.1996)
Dr David.G.Long (R.B.G. Edinburgh)
Dr Henry Noltie (R.B.G. Edinburgh)
Dr Sinha (B.S.I.Gangtok)
Usha Lachungpa (Sikkim Forestry Dept)
Sonam Wangchuk (Bhutan Forestry Dept)
David Lang
Ganden Lachungpa (trekking organiser)
Tashi Lachungpa (trekking assistant)

Lakhpa Tsering (mountaineer)
Suren Sunar (cook)
Gut Lepcha (Forestry Department)
Bhuvan Pradhan (forestry department)
Kumar Sewa (assistant)

A Sikkim Odyssey 2001
(30.8.2001–29.9.2001)
Dr Paramjit Singh (B.S.I. Gangtok)
Mohan Pradhan (Sikkim Conservation)
David Lang
Ganden Lachungpa (trekking organiser)
Gyapo Bhutia (cook)
Siwa Mukhia (assistant)
Prakash Gurung (assistant)
Kumar Sewa (assistant)
Sonam (local guide)
Yamphel (local guide)

Index

(illustrated entries indicated in **bold**)

Cymbidium eburneum [Mohan Pradhan]

198

Pleione praecox